TRUE STORY: A TRILOGY

plays by Dan O'Brien

The Body of an American
The House in Scarsdale
New Life

DALKEY ARCHIVE PRESS
Dallas / Dublin

ISBN Paperback: 978-1-628975-13-0
Library of Congress Cataloging-in-Publication Data: Available

Cover design by Anna Jordan
Interior design by Anuj Mathur

Dalkey Archive Press

www.dalkeyarchive.com
Dallas, TX/Rochester, NY

Printed on permanent/durable acid-free paper.

Table of Contents:

Table of Contents:

INTRODUCTION

These plays tell the truth. Or they try to anyway.

The Body of an American began with a war reporter named Paul Watson on NPR's *Fresh Air* in August of 2007. I was leaving an idyllic year-long residency at Princeton University, leaving also the aspiring phase of my career as a playwright in New York City, and moving with my new wife to our uncertain future in Los Angeles. The so-called "war on terror" was at its nadir. My family had recently disowned me without explanation. When I heard Paul Watson's voice on the podcast in my earbuds, I was disturbed by what his voice retained: the trauma of war, which intriguingly seemed to rhyme or chime with the comparatively minor trauma of my childhood. We spent more than two years emailing each other, getting to know each other, learning to trust each other, before finally meeting face to face at the beginning of the end of winter in the Canadian High Arctic. My docudrama about the ghosts of war, derived from Paul's memoir, his reportage, our correspondence, and recordings of our conversations, became in the end a story about friendship and the possibility of healing through the witnessing of pain.

My collaboration with Paul Watson wasn't finished, however; in the years that followed I wrote two collections of poetry about him, as well as the libretto for an opera. I planned to write another play about Paul but first I needed to take a detour. Working with him had taught me to question and I wanted to investigate my childhood like a journalist. *The House in Scarsdale* is adapted from interviews with some of my many estranged relatives, as I sought to solve the mystery of my family's unhappiness. One prospective answer compelled me: might my father's brother be my actual father? Without the excuse of the play's research and composition, the scaffolding of its narrative, the projection of myself as a character, I would have never summoned the courage to contact these ghosts from my past.

As I was conceiving of another play about Paul, the conclusion in what I was considering a trilogy, my wife was diagnosed with cancer, and six months later I was diagnosed with cancer too. This was 2015 and 2016. What had been envisioned as a play about Paul's experiences in Iraq and Afghanistan and Syria, and his desire to retire from journalism in order to repurpose his trauma as a "prestige" cable TV drama series, became instead (or additionally) a play about the catastrophe of cancer. This was not the conclusion I had imagined. I wasn't going to be able to accompany Paul to Kandahar, for example, as had been my plan; instead my task was to survive nine months of surgeries and chemotherapy treatments. *New Life* was written on the rare days between infusions when I was strong enough to sit at my desk and type, when I wondered if this would be the last play I ever wrote—if I would even finish.

———————

I used to write fictionally. That had been the point. Storytelling was an egress from real-ity—or more accurately a strategy for telling the truth about myself and my family in a code that my family could not decipher. And if they did recognize themselves, well, at least I had plausible deniability. I was disguising myself too, of course: wearing the mask of fiction I could expose secrets without taking full responsibility for it.

But being disowned changed all that. I felt lost; I felt free. Fiction now seemed friv-olous, evasive. I felt compelled to be honest with myself, and with my audience. A true story was suddenly superior to anything I might dream up on my own. Maybe fiction was vain? Life, if one is looking and listening closely, is the revelation.

That said, a true story may not be what the audience wants. The audience wants some version of diversion, and who can blame them? But I wanted to confront the audience, insofar as I hoped that these plays could confront denial: denial of the disasters of the wars in Iraq and Afghanistan and Syria; denial of mental illness, familial cruelty, and transgenerational trauma; and denial of illness and mortality. This last subject, the last play in my trilogy, has proved a hard sell. *New Life* was receiving readings and workshops at theaters before the COVID pandemic, but nothing since. It may remain that com-monplace casualty known as the unpremiered play, and maybe for good reason, but I am publishing it in the spirit again of speaking my mind about trauma, even if the story is unpopular. Or because it is unpopular.

Speaking of unpopular: why are these plays written in verse?

For the record, each line contains ten syllables, with some wiggle room for variation in pronunciation (to say nothing of the occasional miscount). Meter is only acciden-tally—and conversationally—iambic. The verse isn't intended to communicate loftiness or pretentiousness to readers, performers, or audiences. In fact in performance I don't believe audiences are unduly aware of any conspicuous "poetry" in these plays. I simply found it helpful to write with this restriction, or really a tension between the mess of existence and the artifice of verse, and by extension the artifice of the stage. Writing with the obsessional care of a poet was like mining the pages and pages of journalism and prose, and the hours and hours of audio and video recordings, for the gold vein of drama.

Another caveat: these plays are strange. Because reality, observed stringently, is strange to me. Certainly the ordeal of trauma estranges one from oneself. The multiplicity of identity in these plays evokes the dissociative fracturing of post-traumatic stress disorder; two actors who are usually two characters who are intermittently, shockingly inhabited by other characters—this is how moral injuries reverberate in the psyches and bodies of witnesses and survivors. The conceit is unabashedly theatrical—some have called it "exper-imental"—but my intention is to disabuse the audience of the illusion of the familiar in pursuit of a more scrupulous portrayal of life.

Somehow *New Life* was not my last play. But it was the end of writing plays in this way. Paul Watson and I are still friends, but I don't write about him anymore, and I suspect he's happy about that. I am no longer bothered much by the loss of my family. My wife and I are healthy, though we take nothing for granted. I sit typing at my desk again, often joyously, baffled by my state of grace.

And I am again writing fictionally, but not like I used to. I allow myself the luxury of invention, writing speculative plays with a core of truth, and truthful plays elaborated with imagination—that is to say, with empathy. I am thankful for the decade collected here, a time when I was required to cast a cold eye on what was real in my history, in our history, before I could move on to something truly new.

March 2023
Los Angeles

THE BODY OF AN AMERICAN

Inspired in part by the memoir Where War Lives

by Paul Watson

The Body of an American was the winner of the Horton Foote Prize for Outstanding New American Play, the inaugural Edward M. Kennedy Prize for Drama, the PEN Center Award for Drama, and the L. Arnold Weissberger Award. The play was commissioned and developed with support from The Playwrights' Center's McKnight Commission and Residency Program, Minneapolis, MN. Additional support was received from the Rockefeller Foundation Bellagio Residency, a Future Collaborations Grant from Theatre Communications Group, a Sundance Institute Time Warner Storytelling Fellowship, PlayLabs at The Playwrights' Center, the New Harmony Project, and a workshop at Pioneer Theatre.

The Body of an American premiered off-Broadway in 2016 at the Cherry Lane Theatre, a co-production of Primary Stages, Andrew Leynse, Artistic Director, and Hartford Stage, Darko Tresnjak, Artistic Director.

Cast
PAUL: Michael Cumpsty
DAN: Michael Crane

Creative Team
Director: Jo Bonney
Dramaturg: Elizabeth Williamson
Scenic Design: Richard Hoover
Costume Design: Ilona Somogyi
Lighting Design: Lap Chi Chu
Sound Design: Darron L. West
Projection Design: Alex Basco Koch
Casting: Binder Casting/Jack Bowdan, CSA

The Body of an American received its European premiere in 2014 at the Gate Theatre in London, Christopher Haydon, Artistic Director, in co-production with Royal & Derngate, Northampton, James Dacre, Artistic Director.

Cast
PAUL: William Gaminara
DAN: Damien Molony

Creative Team
Director: James Dacre
Design: Alex Lowde
Lighting Designer: Charles Balfour
Sound Designer: Adrienne Quartly
Video Design: Dick Straker for Mesmer

The world premiere of *The Body of an American* was produced in 2012 by Portland Center Stage, Portland, OR, Chris Coleman, Artistic Director, after having received a workshop at JAW: A Playwrights Festival at Portland Center Stage.

Cast
PAUL: William Salyers
DAN: Danny Wolohan

Creative Team
Director: Bill Rauch
Scenic and Costume Designer: Christopher Acebo
Lighting Designer: James F. Ingalls
Sound and Projections Designer: Eamonn Farrell
Sound Designer: Casi Pacilio
Dialect Coach: Mary McDonald-Lewis
Stage Manager: Jeremy Eisen
Production Assistant: Kailyn McCord

Characters:

Two actors play all the roles: ideally an actor in his 30s who plays Dan most of the time, and an actor around 50 to mostly play Paul.

The older actor has the first line of the play, and with each new character heading—even when it's the same character—the actors alternate.

Place & Time:

Scenes 1-7: various.

Scenes 8-10: the Arctic, 2010 and various.

Notes:

The right-hand column of the script contains suggestions of photographs, video, maps, etc., to be projected somewhere prominent onstage, as well as suggestions of light and sound. All of the photographs and video listed are by Paul Watson or the playwright or unknown, except where noted.

Running time is 90-100 minutes without an intermission.

For Isobel Kelly

For Isobel Kelly

I do want to hear this because
you're another person in this story.
Um, and each, each person in this story
ends up telling his own story of what
I call—the working title for the book
I'm writing is *Where War Lives*. From a quote
of Albert Camus when he was keeping
his notebooks pre-World War Two. And a friend
wrote to him saying, you know, I'm grappling
with this philosophical question, Where
does this vile thing, war, live? And Camus said,
he's in Algiers at the time and he says,

I look at the bright blue sky and I think
of the guilt that I feel from not being
in a position where I, I can die
with them, while at the same time wanting to
be as far away as I can from it.

—Paul Watson in conversation with Dr. Joseph LeDoux, January 2006

1: FRESH AIR

PAUL:	My name's Paul Watson.
PAUL:	I'm Paul Watson.
TERRY GROSS:	This is *Fresh Air*,
TERRY GROSS:	I'm Terry Gross. Remember that famous 1993 photo?
PAUL:	I was a reporter who happened to—
DAN:	Dear Mr. Watson. I don't usually email strangers like this.
TERRY GROSS:	This is *Fresh Air*.
DAN:	I was leaving Princeton.
PAUL:	New Jersey?
DAN:	Where I had this fellowship.
PAUL:	You had a what?
DAN:	A residency—
PAUL:	Which means you do what?
DAN:	Well I was supposed to write a play.
PAUL:	A play.
DAN:	Yes.
PAUL:	About what?
DAN:	Ghosts.
PAUL:	Ghosts?
DAN:	Yeah. Ghosts.
PAUL:	What kind of ghosts?
DAN:	Historical, ghosts.
PAUL:	And they pay you for this?
DAN:	Sort of. Definitely. I'm really grateful to them—
PAUL:	Is it scary?
DAN:	My play? I don't know. I hope so. To me it was.
TERRY GROSS:	This is *Fresh Air*,
TERRY GROSS:	I'm Terry Gross. Let's start

                              with a description of that now famous
                              Pulitzer prize-winning photo:
PAUL: I was
                              a reporter who happened to carry
                              a camera, a 35 mm
                              Nikon I bought because my editors
                              wouldn't buy me one.
PAUL: We were on the roof
                              of the Sahafi, where the journalists were
                              staying,
PAUL: *if* they were staying.
PAUL: You could count
                              on one hand who was still there.
PAUL: I'd have to
                              count on one hand because my other hand
PAUL: isn't really a hand at all.
PAUL: I was
                              born this way.
PAUL: A bunch of us were drinking
                              beer.
PAUL: Did you see that light?
REPORTER: What light?
PAUL: Behind
                              that chopper there. It just went down behind
                              that hill.
DAN: Chaos ensues.   *Image: white light.*
PAUL: A 16-hour
                              battle raged through the night between US
                              Army rangers, special ops, Delta Force
                              and Somali militias. It started
                              as an arrest operation trying
                              to abduct commanders in Mohamed
                              Aideed's militia. They were trying to
                              track down Aideed and arrest him for
                              allegedly organizing attacks
                              on UN peacekeepers.
PAUL: When I woke up
                              on the hotel floor, still dressed, hung over,
PAUL: 18 American soldiers had been killed
                              and 75 wounded.
PAUL: Clouds of smoke
                              billowing up from burning tire barricades,
                              dead bodies in the street.
PAUL: American troops
                              were trying to get the rest of their force

back alive, and in so doing they'd killed
more than 600 Somalis so far,

PAUL: including women and children, huddled
in the darkness as bullets or shrapnel
pierced the tin walls of their shacks.

PAUL: Gutale's
my translator. He hurries through the gate:

GUTALE: They are shooting everything that moves now,
even donkeys!

PAUL: He gets 30 dollars
a day.

PAUL: My driver and bodyguard get
a hundred.

PAUL: That's always been the hardest
part of my job: convincing good people
who get none of a byline's ego boost
to risk their lives because I've decided
a story's worth dying for.

GUTALE: They're shooting
people on sight! Even people with no
weapons!

PAUL: Mogadishu was beautiful
once, white-painted Italianate villas
in the capital of the most stable
state in Africa.

PAUL: Now you see women
grocery shopping with militias firing
machine guns up and down the avenue,

PAUL: children playing on the front lines, running
water and bullets beside their mothers
to keep the gunmen supplied.

GUTALE: They shot down
a Black Hawk! They are taking a soldier
with them from street to street, perhaps alive,
perhaps dead!

PAUL: They threw me in the back seat
of the car,

PAUL: a Toyota Cressida
that nobody outside of the safe zone
would recognize,

PAUL: and made me hide my face
between Gutale and my body guard
Mohamed.

PAUL: With another Mohamed
driving, and a gunman in front cradling

	an AK-47,
PAUL:	we drove through
	the gates and crawled from street to street. Passing
	the corpse-collectors, men carrying bodies
	by their hands and feet, glaring at us through
	the filthy windshield.
GUTALE:	Has anyone seen
	a captured American soldier?
PAUL:	Some said,
GUTALE:	They've seen him. He says he's alive, tied up
	in a wheelbarrow.
PAUL:	A wheelbarrow?
GUTALE:	No,
	this man says he's dead. He's most definitely
	dead.
PAUL:	I took a few pictures of some kids
	bouncing up and down on a rotor blade
	in the smoldering tail section of that downed
	Black Hawk.
GUTALE:	Have you seen the American
	soldier?
PAUL:	The entire crowd pointed,
GUTALE:	This way.
PAUL:	Each time a Black Hawk thundered past people
	would shake their fists and curse at it.
PAUL:	We drove
	all over the city for two hours and
	were about to give up,
PAUL:	when the driver
	makes a u-turn.
GUTALE:	He sees something.
PAUL:	A mob
	of 200 Somalis, moving down
	an alleyway.
GUTALE:	What is it?
MOHAMED:	This is bad,
	too dangerous.
GUTALE:	Go slowly.
PAUL:	What's he saying?
GUTALE:	He's a coward. He's worried about his
	car.
MOHAMED:	This guy's going to get us killed!
GUTALE:	Shut up!
PAUL:	Gutale gets out:
GUTALE:	Gamay's in the car,

PAUL:
back alive, and in so doing they'd killed
more than 600 Somalis so far,
including women and children, huddled
in the darkness as bullets or shrapnel
pierced the tin walls of their shacks.

GUTALE: Has anyone seen
a captured American soldier?

PAUL: Some said,

GUTALE: They've seen him. He says he's alive, tied up
in a wheelbarrow.

PAUL: A wheelbarrow?

GUTALE: No,
this man says he's dead. He's most definitely
dead.

PAUL: I took a few pictures of some kids
bouncing up and down on a rotor blade
in the smoldering tail section of that downed
Black Hawk.

GUTALE: Have you seen the American
soldier?

PAUL: The entire crowd pointed,

GUTALE: This way.

PAUL: Each time a Black Hawk thundered past people
would shake their fists and curse at it.

PAUL: We drove
all over the city for two hours and
were about to give up,

PAUL: when the driver
makes a u-turn.

GUTALE: He sees something.

PAUL: A mob
of 200 Somalis, moving down
an alleyway.

GUTALE: What is it?

MOHAMED: This is bad,
too dangerous.

GUTALE: Go slowly.

PAUL: What's he saying?

GUTALE: He's a coward. He's worried about his
car.

MOHAMED: This guy's going to get us killed!

GUTALE: Shut up!

PAUL: Gutale gets out:

GUTALE: Gamay's in the car,

you know Gamay!

PAUL: Gamay is local slang
for cripple.

GUTALE: Quiet man! No hand! He's not
American, he's Canadian! You know
Gamay. He just wants to take some pictures.
Can he?

PAUL: The crowd parts around me.

PAUL: I look
down at the street:

PAUL: and I meet Staff Sgt.
William David Cleveland.

GUTALE: Take the picture
quickly.

PAUL: I've taken pictures of corpses
before, many of them much more fucked up
than this man.

GUTALE: Hurry, Paul!

PAUL: I bend over,
shoulders stiff.

GUTALE: Take it now!

PAUL: With a camera
in front of your eye, you cover your face
and you focus only on the good shot.

PAUL: You shut everything else out.

PAUL: Everything
goes quiet.

PAUL: Despite the noise of the crowd
and the helicopters,

PAUL: everything goes
completely silent. And I hear a voice
both in my head and out:

CLEVELAND: If you do this,
I will own you forever.

PAUL: I'm sorry
but I have to.

CLEVELAND: If you do this, I will
own you.

PAUL: I've sought psychiatric treatment
in subsequent years. And my psychiatrist
says it's my superego. I believe
it was William David Cleveland speaking
to me.

TERRY GROSS: And what did he mean?

PAUL: Well, Terry,

I took it as a warning.

TERRY GROSS: A warning
of what exactly?

PAUL: I have to do this.

PAUL: I don't want to do this.

PAUL: I don't want to
desecrate your body.

CLEVELAND: If you do this
I will own you forever.

PAUL: I took his
picture.

PAUL: While they were beating his body
and cheering. Some spitting.

PAUL: Some kid wearing
a chopper crewman's goggles shoves his way
into the frame. His face is all screwed up
in rapturous glee while giving the dead man
the finger.

PAUL: An old man's raising his cane
like a club and thudding it down against.
the dead flesh.

PAUL: Wind's blowing dirt and the stench
is making me gag.

PAUL: For weeks I'd hated
UN peacekeepers like this man, who killed
from the sky with impunity.

PAUL: But now
it was us against them.

GUTALE: Get in the car,
Gamay!

PAUL: The men holding the ropes that bind
the soldier's wrists are stretching his arms out
over his head.

PAUL: They're rolling his body
back and forth in the hammering morning light.

PAUL: I feel like I'm standing beside myself.

PAUL: I feel like I'm somebody else watching
myself take these photographs,

PAUL: somebody
named Paul, doing this crazy thing,

PAUL: shooting
pictures.

PAUL: Asking, Did I put the batteries
in?

PAUL: *Click.*

*Image: Paul Watson's
full-length photograph
of Staff Sgt. William
David Cleveland.*

*Image: another shot
from this series.*

Image: another shot

PAUL: The bullet wounds are in his legs: *from this series.*
                 did they shoot him in the street, did he die
                 before he crashed?
PAUL: *Click.*   *Image: another shot.*
PAUL: His body's so limp
                 he must have just died.
PAUL: *Click.*   *Image: another shot.*
PAUL: Maybe he's still
                 alive? Is that why I can hear his voice?
                 If you do this,
PAUL: *Click. Click.*   *Image: another shot.*
PAUL: I will own you.
PAUL: *Click. Click. Click. Click.*   *Image: another shot.*
PAUL: You poor man. Who are you?
GUTALE: We must go. Let's go. They don't want us here
                 anymore.
PAUL: The car door's shut.
PAUL: Soft idling
                 of the engine. The muffled mob.
PAUL: It's like
                 I've stepped out of Mogadishu into
PAUL: a wobbling canoe years ago in   *Moving image: water*
                 Sudan,   *at dusk.*
PAUL: drifting downriver at dusk with
ANDREW: Andrew Stawicki,
PAUL: a Polish émigré
                 photographer who snaps a picture of
                 boys running naked like a snake along
                 the river's blood-red spine. That's going to be
                 a great picture.
ANDREW: They won't print it.
PAUL: Why not?
ANDREW: The kid's dick is showing!
PAUL: In my mind's eye
                 I see Sgt. Cleveland's Army-issue
                 green underwear, the only clothing left
                 on his body.
PAUL: The underwear's slightly   *Image: Paul's full-body*
                 askew, so you can just make out a piece   *shot.*
                 of the dead man's scrotum.
PAUL: Open the door!
                 Open it!
PAUL: This time I framed it better:
                 the body from the waist up.
PAUL: A woman   *Image: Paul's famous*

| | slapping him with a flattened can. | *half-body shot.* |

PAUL: That boy
with the goggles shoveling his face through
the mob,

PAUL: laughing at us.

PAUL: Men with bloodshot
eyes notice me.

PAUL: It would be like squashing
a cockroach to kill me, this infidel
who can't take a hint.

GUTALE: Look, he's leaving now!
See? We're leaving for good! Thank you!

PAUL: The squeak
of the hotel gate always let me breathe
easier. As if a few sleepy guards could
actually keep us safe from everything
happening out there.

PAUL: I take the service stairs
two at a time to my room, stuff the roll
of film between the mattress and box spring,
switch on the broken AC,

PAUL: and collapse
on my bed with my eyes closed and I cry
for a very long time.

TERRY GROSS: This is *Fresh Air.*
The AP printed it, and so did *Time*
magazine.

PAUL: That's right. AP moved the half
-body shots, which appeared in newspapers
all over the world. What *Time* magazine
did, which I find fascinating, is they
digitally altered the underwear
so you can't see any genitals. But
you do see horrific desecration
of an American soldier.

TERRY GROSS: This picture
had incredible impact.

PAUL: Yes, Terry,
that's right. Because immediately the heat
was on President Bill Clinton to do
something. And that something was to announce
the immediate withdrawal of American
troops. Then, when it became time to decide
whether or not the United States should
lead an intervention in Rwanda,

where 800,000 people were killed
in a hundred days, President Clinton
decided not to use the word genocide
so we wouldn't be *forced* to intervene.
And we know without a doubt Al-Qaeda
was there in Mogadishu. It says so
on indictments in US Federal Court,
bin Laden's bragged about it, his minions
have bragged about it. But what disturbs me
the most is that Al-Qaeda learned a lot
from the propaganda impact of that
photograph. 18 American soldiers
were killed that day. Which is nothing compared
to what used to happen on a bad day
in Vietnam. And it's only relatively
bad compared to what's still happening these days
in Iraq, or Afghanistan. I think
it's safe to say, take all of the events
that happened, but remove the photograph,
and Al-Qaeda would not have chased us out
of Somalia, bin Laden would not have
been able to say to his followers, Look
we're able to do this, we only need
small victories to defeat history's greatest
military. After my photograph:
9/11, and this never-ending
war on terror.

TERRY GROSS: My guest today has been
war reporter Paul Watson. His new memoir
about reporting from war zones is called
Where War Lives.

TERRY GROSS: We'll talk more after a break.

2: WHO WAS HE TALKING TO?   *Google map: Princeton, NJ.*

DAN: I was listening to this podcast. Writing
my play about historical ghosts. Packing
up all our things. It was the very end
of August. It was the end of New York
for us. It was the end of something else,
what? our youth? In Princeton. Which is just so
beautiful this time of year. Every time
of year, really. All the trees and leaves. All

the squirrels. All of the privileged children,
including myself, in some ways. I was
sad to leave. It had been a rough few years.
I'd walk around the campus late at night
and feel almost good about myself. Smart.
Of value. And of course I felt guilty
too, to have had this library. These trees
and squirrels. The beautiful young women
to watch. Unlimited laser printing.
While you're off in Iraq, Paul. Or Kabul.
Or Jakarta, that's where you live, Paul, right?   *Google map: Jakarta.*
And Jakarta's in Indonesia. Right?
There was this hangar-sized Whole Foods nearby,   *Video image: verdant*
lots of Priuses, and bumper stickers   *window in Princeton.*
celebrating the date when Bush would leave
office. I'd go running in thunderstorms
sometimes. I'd sit on the back porch sipping
vodka, cooking meat on a charcoal grill.
Watching swallows swoop out of a twilit
sky into my maple tree. And your voice
got to me. It's your voice:

PAUL: I tend to be
solitary.

DAN: This is you speaking, though
it might as well be me.

PAUL: I like to stay
home with my wife and son.

DAN: Dinner parties?

PAUL: I tend to stay away. I've spent enough
time around people who do what I do,
and in my opinion, and I include
myself foremost in this group, we're a bunch
of misfits, people who are seeking self
-esteem through risk.

DAN: I felt you could have been
talking about playwrights. Without any
real risk. You were mad:

PAUL: I'm sick of being
lied to. And I take it as a challenge
to make sure nobody's lying to me.

DAN: I felt like I knew you. Or I was you
in some alternate reality.

PAUL: Men
start wars because it helps them to make sure
that women aren't laughing at them.

DAN: You
        were funny. Sort of.

PAUL: I'm more comfortable   *Image: Paul Watson*
        with the weak than I am the powerful,   *preparing to take a*
        growing up in this condition.   *photo; his deformed*

DAN: We should   *hand is prominent.*
        talk about that, your hand.   *(Andrew Stawicki)*

PAUL: Should we?

DAN: Why not?

PAUL: It's helped me out a lot. In Kosovo
        in food lines, they'd think I was a wounded
        war vet and give me all kinds of free stuff.

DAN: And as I'm packing and listening to you
        I'm wondering if I feel so moved because
        you sound so messed up,

PAUL: If something's risky
        and we probably shouldn't do it, I'll say,
        Don't worry about me, I'm already
        dead.

DAN: Or because you scare me. The haunted
        often sound like ghosts, in my experience.

PAUL: I just have this sense I've already lived
        much longer than I should have.

DAN: You poor man,
        who are you?

3: Q&A. OR, GOT TO GO

Photo: Watson Family
photo, 1960; Paul is
in the baby stroller.

PAUL: I have no idea who my father was

DAN: He was a soldier, right?

PAUL: I've got to go.
        Take care. Paul.

DAN: I just wanted to say thanks
        for writing me back. I got your email
        on my wife's BlackBerry halfway across
        the country, at this tumbleweed rest stop
        on an Indian reservation somewhere
        outside Tulsa.

PAUL: Dear Dan, I just got back
        from Kabul. Where I found out it's easy   *Google map: Kabul.*
        to buy stolen US military
        flash drives at an Afghan bazaar outside   *Images: ID photos of*
        Bagram air base. And these flash drives are full   *US soldiers,*

of classified information, social
security numbers of soldiers, maps
of Taliban and Al-Qaeda targets
in both Afghanistan and Pakistan.

*maps of air strikes in
Afghanistan and
Pakistan, 2008.*

DAN: Wow.

PAUL   Sorry, what were we talking about?

DAN: Your dad.

PAUL: Stormed the beach at Normandy. Died
a few days shy of my second birthday.

DAN: And you were born when?

PAUL: 1959.
How old are you, Dan?

DAN: I'm younger than you.
I could be your nephew, or a younger
brother maybe.

PAUL: My father didn't die
in the war though.

DAN: Of course not. How did he?

PAUL: He had PKD, or Polycystic
Kidney Disease.

DAN: Which is what?

PAUL: Like it sounds:
cysts start growing all over your kidneys
till eventually you die. I have it
too.

DAN: Will it kill you?

PAUL: I've got pills for it.

DAN: So, what you mean when you say you don't know
who your dad was, is you don't remember
him?

PAUL: Do you?

DAN: Do I remember my dad?

PAUL: Do you know who he is?

DAN: What do you mean?

PAUL: What did you think I meant?

DAN: He was around.
I mean my father was always around,
every day. He never spoke to us. If
he did, well then it was just to tell you
how fucking stupid you were.

PAUL: Is he dead?

DAN: I don't know.

PAUL: You don't know?

DAN: Wait why are you
asking *me* questions?

PAUL: I've got to get back
to Kabul. I'll email you.
DAN: I'm staying
in this condo in a renovated
schoolhouse. Sometimes I hear ghostly children
laughing. This gland in my neck is swollen
and aches. I'm Googling the symptoms. Let's Skype
or Facebook. Are you on Facebook?
PAUL: I don't
know why but I'd rather keep emailing
like this. I don't know why. But it's almost
like a conversation.
DAN: Yeah but it's not
a conversation.
PAUL: Yeah but it's almost.
Are you in LA?
DAN: I'm in Madison,   *Google map: Madison,*
Wisconsin.   *WI.*
PAUL: What? Why?
DAN: Teaching.
PAUL: And writing
about ghosts?
DAN: Sure. Still.
PAUL: Is it snowing there?   *Moving image: falling*
DAN: It hasn't stopped snowing since I touched down   *snow.*
in January. Cars are abandoned
in the middle of highways. I don't leave
the condo much.
PAUL: I'm home in Jakarta,   *Moving image:*
in case you're wondering. There's a thunderstorm   *lightning, rain.*
and my little boy's asleep. He's always
asking me, How long will you be gone, Dad?
He's seven, so he doesn't understand
time just yet. Few weeks back we were lying
in bed together and he asked me, When
you're dead will you still be watching me? Where
were we?
DAN: We were talking about fathers.
PAUL: So then Ray enlisted at 17,
DAN: You call him Ray?
PAUL: faked his eye test. He was,
SOMEONE: Tall. Splendid physique.   *Image: family photo*
PAUL: That's what someone wrote   *again; Paul's tall father.*
about him, in one of his files. It said,
Ray is:

SOMEONE: Frank. Pleasant manner. Decisive
style of thinking.

PAUL: This one story I know,
there's only one story I know for sure,
they were taking a medieval city
in France, twisted streets, churches and houses   *Map: Villonsles-*
made of stone. My father takes a bullet   *buissons, France,*
in his thigh. Watches one of his soldiers   *1944.*
trapped in the long grass. Ray can't do a thing
but watch his friend die. Each time this man cries
out for help, a Nazi sniper shoots him
till he's dead.

DAN: How do you know this?

PAUL: Research.
My mother told me.

DAN: Yes. Good. What's she like?

PAUL: She's the strongest woman I know.

DAN: Okay—

PAUL: I've got to cut this one short.

DAN: Can we talk
about your hand again?

PAUL: My hand?

DAN: You know,
your lack of a hand.

PAUL: I'll be in Sulu,
in the Philippines.

DAN: Outside my window   *Moving image: snow*
a freight train rolls past every night. Its bell   *falling.*
tolls over and over again,

PAUL: Seven
civilians have been killed by Philippine
troops, including two children.

DAN: as the snow
piles higher on Lake Monona, burying
the sign Obama stuck in the ice: *Yes
We Can!*

PAUL: Reading glasses, check. Sensible
shoes, check.

DAN: Spring break.   *Image: bright light.*

PAUL: Hey, Dan! You were asking
about my hand. It doesn't bother me
much. My mother used to always tell me,
Nobody's perfect!

DAN: How'd it get that way?

PAUL: The kids would crowd around me at recess

and the bravest ones would reach out and touch
my stump,

KIDS: How'd it get that way, Paul? Huh? Huh?

PAUL: This was when I remember first thinking:
This is not me.

PAUL: This, that body belongs
to somebody else.

PAUL: The day I was born
I had these nubbins instead of fingers

PAUL: and the doctor just snipped them off.   *Image: that picture
                                                                  again of Paul preparing*

PAUL: The hand's   *to take a photograph.*

attached to a wrist that bends, with a palm   *(Stawicki)*
no bigger than an infant's.

DAN: Did your mom
take thalidomide?

PAUL: Everyone thinks that,
but no she didn't. It's a mystery,
something in the DNA.

DAN: Is that why
you're like this?

PAUL: Like what, Dan?

DAN: Oh I don't know,
a war reporter?

PAUL: iPod, check. Satellite
phone, check. Laptop, check. Endless tangles of
cable, check.

DAN: Two people have been murdered
near where I'm staying,

PAUL: Some bars of Dettol,   *Image: Joel Anthony*
disinfectant soap for microbes.   *Marino.*

DAN: a man
my age. A girl. On different days.

PAUL: Check.

DAN: Both   *Image: Brittany*
were stabbed repeatedly. In the middle   *Zimmermann.*
of the day, at home. I go out running
on the icy roads past their stained faces
on telephone poles. Just like I used to
jog past the makeshift morgue outside Bellevue
that long-ago September.

PAUL: Sorry, Dan,
I've been out of touch. I was in Christchurch
on vacation. Where were we?

DAN: Your perfect
childhood.

PAUL: Yes, my street was Princess Margaret   *Google map: Princess*
                 Boulevard, my school was Princess Margaret   *Margaret Blvd.,*
                 Public School.   *Etobicoke, Ontario,*
DAN: Who's Princess Margaret again?   *Canada.*
PAUL: We had a milkman, mailman, paperboy.
DAN: How many siblings did you have?
PAUL: Four. You?
DAN: Five.
PAUL: Wow, you really are Irish!
DAN: Nothing
                 bad happened in your childhood? other than
                 your absent father and your absent hand
                 that never bothered you?
PAUL: Oh, there was one
                 thing that was somewhat disturbing: our friend
                 Andy blew his brains out at his parents'
                 summer cottage.
DAN: Just somewhat disturbing?
PAUL: It was hardly surprising. He was stuck
                 outside himself.
DAN: Were you, Paul?
PAUL: I hung out
                 with this dealer, he must've been 30.
                 At a motel he pulls out a bottle
                 and a baggie full of pills. Up or down,
                 my choice. I wash down a few with a belt
                 of whiskey.
DEALER: You took some heavy downers,
                 man.
PAUL: Who cares?
DEALER: That's the trouble with chicks, right?
PAUL: Right!
DEALER: Hells yeah!
PAUL: An hour later he's carving
                 his arm with his knife.
DEALER: Bitches always want
                 perfection!
PAUL: Then he's slinging my body
                 over his back like I'm some medevaced
                 soldier on TV in Vietnam. Dumping
                 me in a taxi.
DEALER: He's my little bro,
                 man. Just take him home.
PAUL: Alone and puking
                 through the chain link of a construction site

as the taxi spits gravel.

DAN: You were fucked   *Image: close-up of that*
up, Paul. Maybe you were depressed. Maybe   *photo of Paul as a*
you were low on some brain chemical like   *teenager in the '70s.*
serotonin, dopamine, whatever,
and this kind of crazy behavior was
your way of feeling normal.

PAUL: But I was
also having fun. Didn't you have fun
in high school, Dan?

DAN: Sorry, I've got to go
teach. My students are trying to learn how
to write with conflict and stakes and something
remotely real.

PAUL: I had this one teacher
I loved. He took us all on a field trip
once. There we were floating in our canoes   *Moving image: river*
in Algonquin Provincial Park, under   *at night. Stars.*
a canopy of stars. With my classmate
Stephen Harper, future Prime Minister,
no kidding, paddling behind. Thinking, Who
could not love Albert Camus? And that's how
I ended up winning the Pulitzer.

DAN: Wait. What? I don't get it—

PAUL: I've got to go,
this time it's an emergency. Turn on   *Google Map: Burma.*
your TV and you'll see.

DAN: I've got to say,
Paul, I can't help feeling you're not being
entirely honest with me here. I mean,
I don't mean that you're lying, per se. But
everything has this kind of Hemingway
patina to it. This kind of old school
journalistic swagger. It's like you're trying
to impress me.

PAUL: I got into Burma
on a tourist visa. With the Tribune
execs measuring the column inches
we produce, not getting into Burma
to cover the cyclone devastation
would've been career suicide. Hiding
by day in the hull of a riverboat
in the Irrawaddy Delta. Among
the hundreds of corpses bobbing at dusk
in the sea-soaked paddies is the body

of a child. In pajama bottoms with   *Image: this image.*
teddy bear cartoons on them. The bleached skin's
like rotting rattan. The leg bones are green.
The stench is unbearable, but the people
on shore don't seem to notice. My fixer
explains that Buddhists believe the body   *Moving image: river*
FIXER: is nothing more than an empty vessel,   *at night. Stars.*
and the soul has already been reborn
as someone new.

PAUL: After several stiff drinks
that night I lay on the roof of our boat
staring up at the universe,

PAUL: listening
to Laura Bush give forth with earnest pleas
to the junta on Voice of America,

PAUL: and I imagined myself as nothing
more than a passenger on this rotting
vessel of my body. And it felt good,
I felt free.

DAN: That freight train's approaching fast,
its headlamp swallowing the churning snow.
The chiming bell, the shrieking horn—

PAUL: Dear Dan,
I've been meaning to say: you sound kind of
depressed. Don't let that get ahold of you.
Trust me. Maybe you should talk to someone
besides me? Or take a pill. Has it stopped
snowing yet?   *Moving image: falling*
DAN: Nope.   *snow.*
PAUL: Medication. Calculate
estimated time away, multiply
by seven pills a day for depression,
blood pressure, PKD. Toss in extra
in case I get kidnapped. Check.

DAN: Where are you
going this time, Paul?

PAUL: A few chocolate bars:
85 percent cocoa, for the dose
of flavonoids the TV doctor says
will give me an extra 3.5 years
and fight heart plaque.

DAN: Where are you now?
PAUL: My son
is sleeping. It's the rainy season here
again and lightning's lighting up his face

like a strobe. I lean in close to his ear
and whisper,

PAUL: Don't be afraid.

PAUL: I'll come back
home soon.

PAUL: Do not be afraid.

PAUL: Japanese
green tea for the antioxidants. Corkscrew
for the cheap Bordeaux I'll purchase en route
at Duty Free,

DAN: I've got some more questions
for you, Paul—

PAUL: more antioxidants and
some liquid courage to help ease the pain
of these five-star hotel room blues.

4: THE GHOSTS ARE GETTING CLOSER

But I'm whining, Dan.

DAN: Okay, let's get back
to the story. You win the Pulitzer
Prize.

PAUL: I was in Rwanda when I heard
the news. As everybody's aware now,
300 Tutsis an hour were being
beaten to death with these large wooden clubs
with bent nails and heavy spikes sticking out
of them. Real prehistoric shit. Homemade
machetes. Just a few thousand UN
soldiers with air support could've washed all
those maggots away.

PAUL: We were getting high   *Moving image, sound:*
on the bridge over Rusumo Falls.   *waterfall.*

PAUL: We
is not the royal we, we is someone
I don't want you to meet just yet.

PAUL: Khareen
and I watching refugees spill over
the border to Tanzania. Watching
corpses spill over the waterfall down
into this brown whirlpool, smashing against
the rocks.

PAUL: In a house we found children piled   *Sound: flies buzzing.*

like sandbags on a bed.

PAUL: There's a baby
down at the bottom. Its tiny hand is
bloated, its severed head cracked open like
an eggshell. Did the older children try
to hide him in here?

PAUL: Outside the back door
I slipped on a bunch of school books. One book
had been covered neatly with a color
publicity shot of the *Dynasty*
TV show cast. With John Forsythe's fucking
grinning face.

PAUL: The ghosts are getting closer.

PAUL: In Gahini, a 16-year-old named
François Sempundu sat on the grimy
brown foam of his hospital bed.

TRANSLATOR: He says
Hutus hacked up his mother and siblings.
He says he hid beneath the kitchen sink
for a week, beside his family's rotting
corpses.

PAUL: François Sempundu was speaking
so calmly.

TRANSLATOR: He says, By then if someone
had come to kill me I wouldn't have cared
much.

PAUL: At a church near Nyarubuye   *Sound: cicadas,*
we pushed open a gate on a courtyard   *crickets.*
like Auschwitz. Like Sarajevo. They'd come here
hoping God would protect them somehow, but
it only made things that much easier
to get butchered.

PAUL: In Zaire a girl stands
at the roadside. Rows of buzzing corpses.

PAUL: At a Rwandan refugee camp.

PAUL: She's
looking for the toilet,

PAUL: which was a field
where a hundred thousand people would shit
and piss and die.

PAUL: This girl stumbles barefoot
into a ditch of bodies, some rolled up
in reed mats. She's looking everywhere and
now she begins to cry.

PAUL: As if hoping   *Sound: this child* somebody will help her.

crying, as if
far away.

PAUL: But nobody's

coming.

PAUL: I thought to myself, This would make

a great picture.

PAUL: This is a beautiful

picture, somehow.

PAUL: I raised my camera, stepped

Image: this child

backwards to frame her with more corpses and

lost among corpses of

I stepped on a dead old woman's arm.

Rwandan refugees

PAUL: It

in Zaire.

snaps like a stick.

PAUL: Then a few days later

I'm at Columbia University's

Low Memorial Library. In this room

like the Parthenon and the Pantheon

confused. Cornucopias of hors d'oeuvres

on aproned banquet tables, wearing tight shoes

and a navy blazer, wool slacks picked out

this morning at Brooks Brothers. John Honderich,

my boss at the *Star*—

HONDERICH: Watson, you don't look

so hot.

PAUL: I guess I just feel bad about

that soldier's family.

HONDERICH: Have you thought about

finding his wife, or his mother? hunting

them down?

PAUL: Had I?

PAUL: Why hadn't I?

PAUL: I win

a Pulitzer in the category

of Spot News Photography.

PAUL: Collecting

my Tiffany crystal paperweight at

the dais. Shaking hands.

PAUL: Kevin Carter,

who just last month was snorting Ritalin

off the floor of my apartment before

rocketing off into the townships,

PAUL: wins

for Feature Photography:

PAUL: a vulture

waiting for a Sudanese girl to die.

PAUL: Always a popular category.

PAUL: Carter comes back to the table:
CARTER: Hear that
                   applause, Watson? I kicked your arse!
PAUL: Two months
                   later I'm back in Rwanda. Honderich
                   calls me on my satellite phone:
HONDERICH: Carter
                   killed himself last night. Parked his pickup truck
                   in Johannesburg, duct-taped a garden hose
                   to the tail pipe. Left a suicide note
PAUL: that I'll paraphrase:
CARTER: I have been haunted so
                   now I'll haunt you.
HONDERICH: Paul?
HONDERICH: Paul?
PAUL: I don't care about
                   him.
PAUL: —Who cares?
PAUL: I don't care!
PAUL: With so many
                   people suffering all over the world
                   who want nothing more than to live—?
PAUL: That man
                   is a coward!
PAUL: If you can't do your job
                   then get out of the way so someone else
                   can.
PAUL: Of course I've wanted to kill myself
                   before. But the truth is I've always lacked
                   the courage.
PAUL: So I tell myself:
PAUL: Just go
                   someplace dangerous. Let somebody else
                   kill you.

5: SHRINKING

GRINKER: O-kay. So. You are 35 years old,
                   you are male. You are a reporter for
                   the *Toronto Star*, and you're stationed here
                   in Johannesburg.
PAUL: You have a real talent   *Image: dark*
                   for stating the obvious.   *bookcase.*

GRINKER: Are you shaking?
PAUL: Am I?
GRINKER: You have sweat all over your face!
PAUL: Let me just catch my breath.
GRINKER: O-kay.
PAUL: It's just
I've never been to a psychiatrist
before.
GRINKER: And what are you scared will happen
to you?
PAUL: I'll lose my edge.
GRINKER: What does that mean,
your edge?
PAUL: Being crazy.
GRINKER: You think I could
cure you of that?
PAUL: Being somewhat crazy
is a requirement in my line of work.
GRINKER: If you leave I won't charge you anything.
You wouldn't be the first to change his mind
about psychiatry. But you called me, Paul,
and told me you've been feeling paranoid—
PAUL: That's not a psychiatric disorder,
in my opinion. People don't deserve
to be trusted.
GRINKER: You are irritable,
small things will make you cry. Interestingly
you deny nightmares. No psychiatric
history prior to this. Congenitally
deformed arm. Don't smoke. Self-medicating
with lots of alcohol, marijuana—
PAUL: Look,
all I want from you is some feel-good pills
to patch me up. "O-kay"?
GRINKER: O-kay. We can
find you something, I'm sure.
PAUL: Thank you.
GRINKER: But first
you'll need to talk to me. Medication
targets symptoms: we will need to target
your soul as well. You find that funny?
PAUL: Yes.
GRINKER: What's your mother like, Paul?
PAUL: She's the strongest
woman I know.

GRINKER: And have you known many
                women?
PAUL: One.
GRINKER: You've known only one woman?
PAUL: I've been in a relationship with one
                woman. On and off. Khareen.
GRINKER: Careen?
PAUL: Ha!
GRINKER: What a name! Tell me, what's this Careen like?
PAUL: She loves rococo art. Homemade knödles
                and beer for dinner.
GRINKER: Ha ha ha! Sounds nice!
PAUL: Her father is this German bureau chief,
                and one time she was sitting on his lap
                in front of me, smiling, with her bare arm
                up around his neck, like this. She's the one
                who needs some therapy, don't you think? She flashed
                her tits at me once down this long hallway
                in her father's condo—I don't know why
                I feel the need to keep talking about
                her father. She's blonde. Great body. Sexy
                voice. Calls me Paulie. She doesn't let me
                have sex with her though. We share a house but
                I pay the rent. I live in a closet
                -sized room off the kitchen. I'm happiest
                on her leash, so to speak. I like to sit
                with her when she takes a bath or lying
                in bed with candles lit, drinking wine or
                smoking a joint, while she gets herself off
                beneath the covers. It's not sex, she says.
                It's only for comfort, Paulie. She likes
                to tell me that. One time she let a guy
                into our yard to watch through the window
                while she fucked some other guy. She described
                this at breakfast, in great detail. She wants
                to be a war reporter, so we went
                to Rwanda where we met a handsome
                aid worker named Laurent. Who was building
                latrines for refugees. And there I was
                with my camera in my one hand. Shooting
                pictures. By that evening she was lying
                in his tent, under his netting, writing
                in her diary. He got a hotel room
                underneath ours. With grenades exploding
                in the shanties and the death squads spreading

                                    through the streets, I call downstairs. She answers
                                    laughing,

KHAREEN: Paulie?
PAUL: We have to go.
KHAREEN: Not now,
                                    Laurent.
PAUL: They're killing people outside.
KHAREEN: Get
                                    off me please, Laurent!
PAUL: He's living with us
                                    here in Johannesburg. They fight and then fuck
                                    all the time.
GRINKER: Why don't we stop for the day.
                                    I'm going to write you a prescription for
                                    450 milligrams of
                                    moclobemide.
PAUL: Okay. Is that good?
GRINKER: No,
                                    that is bad. You're clinically depressed and
                                    you have post-traumatic stress disorder.
                                    It's good that you've come. Do you have someone
                                    at home? Besides that sick woman, of course.
                                    These drugs will take some time to change your brain
                                    chemistry, and we don't want you killing
                                    yourself in the meanwhile.
PAUL: —Do you believe
                                    in ghosts, Dr. Grinker?
GRINKER: Well, I believe
                                    people are haunted.
PAUL: What if I told you
                                    I came to you in the first place because
                                    I'm haunted. Cursed.
GRINKER: I'd ask you some questions
                                    to rule out schizophrenia.
PAUL: I told him
                                    about the picture.
GRINKER: It's famous. It's yours?
PAUL: Then I told him what Cleveland's voice told me.
CLEVELAND: If you do this,
CLEVELAND: I'll own you forever.
GRINKER: That was your superego. Your mind was
                                    simply speaking to itself.
PAUL: I know what
                                    my own mind sounds like. This was somebody
                                    else.

GRINKER: The soldier?
PAUL: I've felt him next to me,
        feared his presence. He's there when I'm asleep
        and when I wake up. He's there whenever
        I'm happy, when I'm having fun or sex
        or watching TV, as if he's saying,
        This cannot last. And of course he's with me
        whenever things go wrong. He's happiest
        when I'm in pain. He'll never go away
        till he gets what he wants from me.
GRINKER: And what
        does he want from you, Paul?

6: IRAQ

PAUL: This was in Mosul in Northern Iraq
        at the beginning of the war. A boy
        was throwing some pebbles at a marine
        humvee, whose .50 caliber machine gun
        was whipping and twisting like a fire hose
        spraying death. And as I'm taking pictures
        a gang of students comes rushing by with
        another student bleeding from a deep
        gash in his face. Somebody makes that sound,
        you know, *click*, like, Take his picture! And while
        I'm switching lenses you can see the switch
        go on in somebody's head. Like, He's white,
        what the hell's he doing here? They throw me
        to the ground, kick me, stone me. Somebody
        sticks his knife in my back and I'm feeling
        the blood pooling in my shirt. I'm holding
        onto my camera while they're stretching out
        my arms, like this, till I'm floating on top
        of the mob. And I'm not trying to be
        cinematic here, but it was like Christ
        on the cross. Cause I had absolutely
        no sense of wanting to live. Or fighting
        back. Protesting my innocence. Crying
        out for mercy. I had this sense of, Well
        we knew this was coming. And here it is.
        But the truth of these places is always
        the same. A dozen people, a dozen
        against a multitude, formed a circle

around me. And we were close to this row
of shops that were closing, and these people
simply pulled the shutters up and shoved me
under. That's when I realize my camera's
gone, the hand's empty, the mob is pounding
on metal. Stabbing their knives through the slits
in the grate. The tea shop owner says, Look
you know I'd really like to help you but
would you mind leaving my tea shop soon? So
I end up in the street again kneeling
in the dirt at the order of some pissed
-off marines, and somehow I convince them
to take me back behind the wire. That's why
I know it's not just my brain, Doctor. Or
my father dying when I was two. Or
this hand. It would be poetic justice
to get butchered by a mob. Remember
what Cleveland said to me: If you do this
I will own you. I just have this feeling
he's thinking, You watched my desecration,
now here comes yours.

7: SOME EMBARRASSING THINGS. OR, THE PLAN

DAN: Dear Paul. It's been a while. Apologies.
                I've finally escaped from the Wisconsin
                winter, and I'm back in my strange new home,   *Google map: Los Angeles.*
                LA. I've just filled my prescription for
                Zoloft. And I'm hoping you're still willing
                to write this play, or whatever it is,
                with me. I know it's been a long time since
                I first reached out to you. Maybe sometime
                I could give you a call?
PAUL: I have to go
                to the Philippines, where Abu Sayyaf
                the local Al-Qaeda affiliate
                is on the march once again. I'm worried
                my editor, who hates me for reasons
                I can't even pretend to comprehend,
                won't like it. It's not the sort of story
                that tends to garner those coveted clicks
                on the *Times'* website.
DAN: It's 75

degrees here and sunny. Women's faces
are slick masks, thanks to Botox. Some men look
embalmed and tan also. I walk my dog
four times a day. The only helicopters
I see here are LAPD circling
over Brentwood like they're still looking for
OJ's white Bronco. While I'm running up
Amalfi to Sunset the Palisades
look more like the hills of South Korea
on *M*A*S*H*. Or Tuscany. Where are you now,
Paul? What's your cell number? Can I call you?
Can I come visit you in Jakarta
soon?

PAUL: I thought you might enjoy hearing this
sound bite directly from the fetid mouth
of our paper's new owner, Sam Zell. Here's
a link: http://gawker.com/
5002815/exclusive
-sam-zell-says-fuck-you-to-his-journalist

Moving image, silent:
http://gawker.com/
5002815/exclusive
-sam-zell-says-fuck
-you-to-his-journalist

ZELL: My attitude on journalism is
simple: I want to make enough money
so I can afford you!

PAUL: And while it's true
I like a gutter-talking billionaire
as much as the next guy, I do wonder
what he's up to. Especially after
publishing a new employee manual
telling us all to question authority
and "push back."

ZELL: I'm sorry, I'm sorry but
you're giving me the classic what I call
journalistic arrogance of deciding
that puppies don't count!

PAUL: With all the chaos
building at the gates in Afghanistan
and Iraq, he's just the sort of leader
I'm not willing to die for.

ZELL: Hopefully
we'll get to the point where our revenue
is so significant we'll be able
to do both puppies *and* Iraq. Okay?
—Fuck you!

PAUL: So if ghostly voices ever
figure into this script, maybe this clip
will make a good one.

DAN: Don't you think it's strange
you've never heard my voice, Paul? I've heard yours
on *All Things Considered*, the *LA Times'*
website. Let's set this trip up now! I won
a grant to come visit you.

PAUL: Hey, congrats
on the grant! I've got a rusted RV
in Bali, we can watch the surf and drink
and discuss genocide. Only problem is
I finally got fired. And my RV
just got crushed by a tree. But have no fear!
I've got an idea.

DAN: My wife's an actress
on a TV show that flopped. We're not sad
about it at all, but everyone thinks
we should be. It's winter, but it's sunny   *Moving image:*
and warm. Every season's the same: sunny   *water at mid-day.*
and warm. I have trouble remembering what
season it is without thinking. The days
get shorter or longer but the sun stays
the same. I go out running on the beach
at dusk. It's beautiful. It's beautiful.
It's beautiful.

PAUL: I'm going to move back home
to Canada, where the plan is I'll work   *Google terrain map:*
for the *Toronto Star* again. Covering   *Canadian Arctic.*
the Arctic aboriginal beat. Shooting
pictures, writing stories, blogging about
life in the midnight sun. Or the noontime
moon. In any case I've been waking up
thankful each morning I won't have to write
another sentence about Al-Qaeda
ever again. Unless Zawahiri's
hiding in some ice cave.

DAN: You have no clue,
Paul, how happy this makes me! You have no
idea how much the ice-and-snow-and-wind
speaks to me, so much more so than the sun
of LA, or Bali. My entire life
I've been obsessed with nineteenth-century
polar exploration. Trapped in the ice
for months, sometimes years. Scurvy, insanity,
cannibalism. It helps me relax
and fall asleep. So maybe I could come
visit you there this winter? And who knows

maybe the Arctic will be the second
act of our play? Cause I have this deadline
coming up—

PAUL: What kind of deadline?

DAN: It's mine
and it's soon. The end of winter. So when
will you give me your God damned phone number
so I can plan this trip?

PAUL: What are they like,
Dan?

DAN: What?

PAUL: Your plays.

DAN: I don't know. Historical,
like I said. I prefer things in books.

PAUL: Why?

DAN: I like things that have already happened
to other people, a long time ago.

PAUL: Why?

DAN: I don't know. I have some ideas but—

PAUL: Like what?

DAN: Well the truth is I'm insecure
around you, Paul. You intimidate me
terribly. You're like this mythic figure,
with your hand, your constant returning to
the underworld of the most nauseating
things in history. Recent history. You've looked
at that which the rest of us won't look at,
or can't look at. You're the type of writer
I've always wished I were. Engaged with life,
people.

PAUL: You don't engage much with people?

DAN: No. I like to seclude myself. Like you
I like to stay away. Sometimes I lay
my head against my dog's head and I think,
You're my best friend. You're my only friend. If
you get sick I'll get a second mortgage
for you. Even though we don't have a first
mortgage yet. We're just renters. I even
like my obsessions but I don't know why
I do. Like I said, I have my theories
but I think they'd be boring to someone
like you.

PAUL: Try me.

DAN: I'm like you, like I said.
Like you I'll sometimes cry for no reason

at all. Or I don't cry for months and months
and months. Like you I see flashbacks. I'm scared
to change that part of me that's craziest,
because if I'm not crazy anymore
how will I do what I do? I'm the same
age you were in Mogadishu, the same
age Sgt. Cleveland was that day. I'm cursed
too, just like you are.

PAUL: But you won't tell me
what's cursing you?

DAN: Because it can't compare
to what you've been through!

PAUL: After my memoir
came out, I'd hear from strangers who'd tell me
the most intimate things about themselves.
Embarrassing. About their lives. They saw
that just like them I had these internal
conflicts. Except you, you didn't confess
anything. Which is probably why I wrote
you back. Do you know that quote of Camus'
where he says he's solved the mystery of where
war lives? It lives in each of us, he said.
In the loneliness and humiliation
we all feel. If we can solve that conflict
within ourselves then we'll be able to
rid the world of war. Maybe. So tell me,
Dan: where does war live in you?

DAN: My family
stopped talking to me, several years ago,
and I have no idea why. That's not true,
I have many ideas but none of them
make sense. I was about to get married
but it wasn't like they didn't approve
of my wife. It had something to do with
the fact that nobody would be coming
from my family because they have no friends.
I mean literally my parents don't have
any friends. They can barely leave the house
and whatever's left of their own families
won't speak to them for reasons I've never
understood. And I'd just written a play
that was the closest I'd come to writing
autobiography. And my brother
was in the hospital again, for God
knows what exactly, depression mostly.

He hadn't spoken to any of us
in years. Which was mostly okay with me
cause like everyone else in my family
I suppose I just wanted to forget
he'd ever existed at all. Maybe
this was all because of him? reminding
my family of what happened years ago
when I was 12 and he was 17,
one Tuesday afternoon in February
walking up the driveway when I noticed
him coming around the house with his back
all pressed with snow, the back of his head white
with snow, and I thought it was so funny
he wasn't wearing a jacket or shoes.
He was barefoot. And by funny I mean
disturbing. I've told this story thousands
of times, I hardly feel a thing. He'd jumped
out of a window, was what I found out
later, and fallen three stories without
breaking a bone. That night my mother cried
in my arms and said, This is a secret
we will take to our graves. I developed
innumerable compulsions, including
counting, hand-washing, scrupulosity
which is the fear that one has been sinful
in word or deed or thought. I was afraid
to leave the house, to touch any surface,
but I hid it so well that nobody
noticed. I was class president. I played
baseball, soccer. I wrote secret poetry.
And eventually I got out and went
to college. And things went coasting along
as well as things can in a family with
an inexplicably cruel father and
a masochistic mother who can't stop
talking about nothing. Logorrhea
is the clinical term, I think. Until
I came home one weekend for a visit
just before my wedding and my father
said I looked homeless. My beard and hair. When
in fact I looked just like other adjunct
professors of writing. But they told me
I looked like a man who'd slit his own throat
soon. They said I looked just like my father's
brother, a man who disappeared after

Moving image: snow falling.

I was born. He was kind, he was funny,
long hair and barefoot in jeans, a hippy
and some kind of artist. The opposite
of my father. I'm the spitting image
of this man, they said. They were terrified
for this reason. There are things you don't know!
my father kept saying, without saying
what it was exactly I didn't know.
My mother and father were both screaming
together, it felt almost sexual.
There are things you don't know! I drove away
and haven't heard from them since. They are dead
to me. And I don't mean that in the way
it sounds, melodramatically. I mean
I can't remember them. And by memory
I mean I can't feel. I have no pictures
of my childhood. It's like my entire life
up until I was 33 happened
to someone else. Someone who's haunting me,
who makes me feel cursed. Makes me feel certain
that yes, they're right, I've failed, something is wrong
with me. I don't know what it is but yes
something is wrong. I've failed, I've failed, I've failed,
I've failed. Only writing and running helps
some. I sit at my desk like a lab rat
clicking on a button that shows me who's
visiting my website. And it doesn't
tell me who's visiting exactly but
it shows your city or town on a map
of the entire world. When I said they don't
talk to me, that wasn't true. I can tell
my mother checks my website at least once
a day. Sometimes twice. It's a compulsion,
I know, but still I like seeing those dots
on the map. But it's nothing! it's nothing
to complain about, it's the sort of thing
everybody has. And nothing compared
to the unspeakable acts of cruelty
you've seen, Paul.

PAUL: Let's get together somewhere
in the Upper Arctic, in 24
-hour darkness, this winter. The hotels there
are like dorms for racist construction crews
from the south, and the costs run high because
everything's flown in. But the ambience

will be just perfect. So let me know when
you'd like to come, and I'll put together
some kind of plan.

8: HI WHAT'S YOUR NAME WHEN ARE YOU LEAVING?

DAN: Sand snow sand snow sand snow sand snow sand snow
            snow snow snow.
DAN: LAX to Vancouver,
            Vancouver to Yellowknife.   *Google Earth:*
DAN: What the hell   *Yellowknife,*
            kind of name is Yellowknife? I've read that   *Northwest Territories,*
DAN: copper in the ground turned the Inuit's   *Canada.*
            knives yellow.
DAN: Yellowknife to Kugluktuk   *Google Earth:*
            by twin turboprop. How do you say that   *Kugluktuk,*
            name again?   *Northwest Territories,*
DAN: Kugluktuk. But I don't know
            Inuktitut.
DAN: What's that?
DAN: Their language.
DAN: Whose?
DAN: The Inuit. Which means simply people
            in Inuktitut.
DAN: I'm getting all this
            information off Wikipedia
            on my new iPhone.
DAN: The flight attendant
DAN: is an Inuit kid, gay, goth, nose ring
            and an attitude.
ATTENDANT: Does anyone want
            this last bottle of water?
DAN: The pilots
            are supposedly Inuit too, though
            the cockpit door's closed the whole way. No one
            speaks over the intercom. A black guy
            dressed all in white shares the aisle with me:
BLACK GUY: What brings you to the North, my mon?
DAN: His voice
            sounds almost Jamaican.
BLACK GUY: True dat, true dat.
            Are you done with your paper, mon?
DAN: Later

I'll find out his name's Isaac, from Ghana,
when Paul's interviewing him.

DAN: His family
immigrated to Yellowknife after
some coup in the '80s.

DAN: An old woman
in traditional clothes, like calico
fringed with coyote fur, her hood hiding
her face,

DAN: doesn't say a word.

DAN: A teenaged
girl with an iPod as we're descending
into Kugluktuk

DAN: taps me on the arm

DAN: and asks me, smiling wide,

INUIT GIRL: Hi what's your name
when are you leaving?

DAN: Grandma and the girl
shuffling across the ice of Kugluktuk
while Isaac and I fly two more hours north   *Google Earth:*
to Ulukhaktok.   *Ulukhaktok.*

DAN: Where the airport is
a room,

DAN: the cab's a van gliding across
a desert of snow.

DAN: Sand snow.

DAN: The cabbie's
white, from Newfoundland, a newfy.

DAN: Which means
he's some kind of Canadian redneck,

DAN: according to Wikipedia.

TAXI DRIVER: Why
don't you drive the taxi eh? Joe asks me.
You know where everyone lives. Everyone
lives in the same flipping place!

DAN: Then he asks
Isaac, probably because he's black:

TAXI DRIVER: Are you
here to teach basketball eh?

ISAAC: No, soccer.

TAXI DRIVER: That'll be ten dollars eh.

ISAAC: I got it
—welcome to the North, my mon!

DAN: The hotel's
a prefab one-story house, corrugated

tin roof, windows for like six rooms.

DAN: Inside   *Image: hallway of*
it smells like Clorox. Inuit women   *hotel in Ulukhaktok.*
scrubbing the deep fryer.

INUIT WOMAN: Hi what's your name
when are you leaving?

DAN: I'm filling out forms
at the front desk, which is just a closet
with a desk inside it. Paul had emailed
might have to share a room. Please God don't
make us share a room. What if he tries to
get in bed with me? What if he kills me
in my sleep? in his sleep? What happens if
he hangs himself in our shower? At least
then I'll have my second act.

PAUL: Are you Dan?
I'm Paul.

DAN: His hair's messed up. He needs a shave.
His thick wool socks are sloughing off.

DAN: Pink eyes,
unfocused.

DAN: There's a deep crease in his face,
between his eyes like it's carved.

DAN: He's wearing
an old sweatshirt with a red maple leaf
on it.

DAN: Who does this man remind me of?

DAN: He's somebody I should know.

DAN: Paul's left hand
is a stub. Like his arm simply runs out
of arm. But he's still got some kind of thumb
at the end. He's rubbing his furrowed brow
with it.

PAUL: How was Eskimo Air?

DAN: Don't look,
Dan.

DAN: Not now.

DAN: Show what kind of man you are

DAN: by not looking at Paul's hand.

DAN: I wonder
what I look like to him?

PAUL: You look a lot
like Jesus. You know that?

DAN: Thanks?

PAUL: You're a real

	tight packer. Wow.	
DAN:	I brought dehydrated	
	food. You wrote me the food sucked so I bought	
	dehydrated organic lasagna	
	at REI in Santa Monica?	
PAUL:	Ooh, I love that stuff!	
DAN:	Let me just finish	
	with this form, and I'll swing by your room.	
PAUL:	Our	
	room. Door's always open.	
DAN:	—Hey!	
PAUL:	Come on in,	
	Dan, have a seat.	*Moving image: gently*
DAN:	So.	*snowing window.*
PAUL:	So.	
DAN:	So here we are	
	finally!	
PAUL:	Finally! I know it's not that much	
	to look at. But these beds are pretty firm.	
	They keep the heat so high you'll want to sleep	
	on top of the blankets, but it's better	
	than bunking in here with some drunk racist	
	construction worker from Edmonton, right?	
DAN:	Right!	
PAUL:	And cell phones don't work. But the wireless	
	is free. In case you want to Skype your wife.	
	I Skype my wife pretty much every night,	
	if you know what I mean. Ha ha ha. —So	
	what do you want to do this week? Because	
	we never really decided, only	
	that you'd come.	
DAN:	And watch you work.	
PAUL:	And watch me	
	interview people. You're going to get bored.	
DAN:	I could interview you. You know, research	
	for the play. If you want.	
INUIT GIRLS:	Hi what's your name	
	when are you leaving?	
DAN:	Two Inuit girls	
	appear in the doorway. Like *The Shining*	
	or something. Selling key chains and lanyards	
	made of sealskin.	
PAUL:	Not now. Go away.	
DAN:	Why	
	are they all asking that, Hi what's your name	

when are you leaving?

PAUL: They're just assuming
we're leaving soon. Like every other white
person they've ever met.

DAN: Is it okay
if I record this?

PAUL: Guess so.

DAN: Do you miss   *Image: bright light.*
Afghanistan, Paul? places like that?

DAN: Sand
snow snow.

DAN: Do you feel you've made a mistake
leaving war reporting behind? It's like
you've been sent away to Siberia
literally. Or is it like a respite?
a reward for everything before?

DAN: But
I don't ask him any of that. Instead
I ask:

DAN: Do you ever get bored up here,
Paul? It must get kind of lonely.

PAUL: That's right,
but I learn a lot of things too.

DAN: Like what?

PAUL: Like you shouldn't ask too many questions
about polar bear hunts, for example.
It's shamanistic. The Inuit still
believe shamans can turn themselves into
spirits, into animals like muskox
and seals and bears. That shamans can become
other people too. All in the pursuit
of exorcising ghosts—   *Moving image: falling*

DAN: Should I tell him   *snow.*
that for weeks I've been having this feeling
when I run that somebody is running
with me?

DAN: Sand sand sand.

DAN: Over my shoulder
in the sun and the sand.

DAN: Who is that man
who's running after me?

DAN: Which reminds me
of that story of Ernest Shackleton
down at the opposite pole, staggering
through a blizzard with his fellow travelers

	starving, delirious,
DAN:	how they kept seeing
	someone with them,
DAN:	how they kept asking,
DAN:	Who
	is that man who walks always beside you?
DAN:	Is Staff Sgt. William David Cleveland
	following me? And what could he possibly
	want from me? I don't say any of this
	to Paul.
DAN:	Snow snow.
DAN:	I don't want him thinking
	I'm too crazy.
PAUL:	Hey, want to watch TV?
DAN:	We could try to track down a shaman.
PAUL:	Who?
DAN:	That's something we could do. This week. Maybe
	he could try to heal you. Ha ha ha.

PAUL: Oh   *Sound: dogs howling*
that reminds me: I'm trying to set up   *far away, chains,*
this dog sled ride with these two Inuit   *wind.*
hunters named Jack and Jerry. 500
dollars but I'll pay them, the *Toronto*
Star will I mean. Do you hear those huskies
howling? They're chained on the ice all their lives.
I don't know how they take it, the boredom   *Moving image:*
I mean. Because you're right, there's definitely *more snow falling,*
a lot of boredom up here. It's supposed   *becoming a blizzard*
to snow tomorrow, but we'll go sledding.   *of white.*
if the weather's any good.

9: BLIZZARD

                                                Light: dark Arctic
Where's the remote? Do you like John Mayer?   *noon.*
I like John Mayer. And Ryan Adams
too. And Queen Latifah. I like to watch
TV with the sound off and just listen   *Moving image: window*
to my iTunes. This okay with you? This   *full of snow.*
sucks. This sucks. There's nothing good on TV!
I usually watch just like sports, hockey
and football, sometimes entertainment news   *Sound: Ryan Adams*
because it's stupid but I love it when   *singing "Rescue Blues"*
celebrities do stupid things. It helps   *low.*

me relax. And I like watching curling
as an Olympic sport. I love hearing
the women's curling team screaming, Harder!
Faster! All of these women with their brooms
that look more like Swiffer WetJets rubbing
some kind of path in the ice for the weight
or the pot or the stone or whatever
screaming, Harder! Faster! As if that does
anything, really! What about this show,
The Bachelor? Have you seen *The Bachelor?* Look,
she's pretending to cry. She's pretending
to cry! What are all these people, actors?
Strippers? She's trying so damn hard to cry
real tears! Harder! Faster! How's it look?

DAN: Looks
bad.

PAUL: It must be gusting up to like, what,
65 an hour?

DAN: My iPhone says that
it's negative 50 out there.

PAUL: Wind chill
included?

DAN: I'm not sure, let's see.

PAUL: Celsius
or Fahrenheit?

DAN: I'm Googling it.

PAUL: I think
Celsius and Fahrenheit become the same
at minus 40 anyway.

DAN: Earlier
Jack the Inuit hunter woke us up
with some coffee.   *Light: dark dawn.*

JACK: Morning, Paul. Morning, Dan.
Looking really bad out there.

DAN: Almost ten
and it's basically sunrise.

JACK: The next time
you come up here you bring me a brand new
skidoo. Okay? Maybe helicopter.

DAN: Before the ban on polar bear hunting
businessmen from Texas would come up here
and Jack would help them track down a mother
bear to shoot. And mount. These rich guys would leave
enormous tips, like snowmobiles.

JACK: Bad news:

can't go out sledding this morning. Jerry's
got the dogs and Jerry's at the doctor's
because he's got like this titanium plate?
in his forehead, from a real bad sled crash
few years back. Ha ha ha. And anyway
Elder says this snow's no good. GPS
can't see shit today. We'll go tomorrow
at nine, Inuit time.

DAN: Inuit time   *Light: mid-afternoon.*
means what, Paul?

PAUL: At least we've got the wi-fi,
and this six-pack of Bordeaux I picked up
in Yellowknife.   *Back to the soundless*
                                                       TV screen.

DAN: I didn't bring any
alcohol. How could I forget to buy
alcohol?

PAUL: You're not bored are you?   *iPod playing music,*

DAN: I was   *John Mayer, "Stop*
hoping at some point we might get back to   *This Train (Acoustic)*
interviewing you?   *(Live)".*

PAUL: I'm an open book,
Dan. Blank slate. No secrets.

DAN: You want to read
our play? I've got a first act but—

PAUL: I can't
figure out my story. Global warming
or the arts. Or corruption. There's something
shady going on here, I can feel it
with the white guys running this place. Kickbacks
or something. Maybe it's better not to
stir things up too much? don't want to end up
dead in a snowdrift, right?

DAN: Paul's popping pills
out of his many-chambered plastic pill
organizer—

PAUL: Depression, blood pressure,
Polycystic Kidney—

DAN: Which reminds me
to take my Zoloft.

PAUL: Oh God I love this   *Light: evening.*
movie.

DAN: That evening it's *The River Wild*.

PAUL: Meryl Streep's on the run, on the river   *iPod plays*
actually ha ha ha, in a rafting   *Queen Latifah's*
boat trying to escape from this psycho   *"Lush Life" low.*

-killer Kevin Bacon. Is this movie
good? or shit. It's shit but Jesus Meryl
Streep is so gorgeous.

DAN: Paul, can I ask you
some questions, maybe during commercial
breaks?

PAUL: Sure. Shoot.

DAN: I'm thinking it would help me
finish our play. Which you're welcome to read
at any point, by the way—

PAUL: Do you want
a glass of Bordeaux?

DAN: Yes please.

PAUL: Go ahead.
Blank book, open slate.

DAN: What is it about
the Arctic—?

PAUL: I guess I'm just happiest
when I'm unhappy. When I'm on the phone
with one of my brothers and he's talking
about, you know, problems at work. I say,
How long we been talking? 15 minutes.
I say: Now you're 15 minutes closer
to death.

DAN: I'm sure he loves that.

PAUL: It bugs me
to the core though! that people don't notice
how quickly we die. Whether you're driving
home from work, or suntanning on a beach
in Phuket and this wave comes in and just
keeps on coming—

DAN: How can you live like that?
I mean, how can you walk around living
like you're going to die? Like back in LA
you can't be worried about the earthquake
that could erupt any second. You can't
ride the New York City subway thinking
about the likelihood of a terrorist
bomb exploding. Like on 9/11
I woke up—

PAUL: You were there?

DAN: And actually
I saw a ghost in our bedroom. Covered
in dust. Carrying his briefcase. He looked
so confused! He disappeared and I heard

the sirens. I went downstairs to find out
what was going on, and to hit Starbuck's
too. All these papers were spiraling down
from the sky. And I remember thinking
for a minute, Now all the bankers will
be humbled. I got my venti latte
and came back out in time to see the plane
hit the second tower. An old woman
sat down on the pavement and just started
sobbing. I went upstairs to get my wife
though we weren't married yet, and we joined
a river of people like refugees
walking uptown. While all the working men
and women were jumping. I never saw
my brother jumping out of the window
of our house, all those years ago. Maybe
there's something in that? A radio outside
a hardware store in Chinatown told us
the South Tower had come down. In a bar
somewhere in the East Village we watched as
the North Tower sank out of the blue sky
on TV. People were almost giddy
with panic, and grief. Some guys were tossing
a Frisbee in the street. I told myself,
If there's going to be a war, I will go.
I saw myself holding a machine gun
in my mind's eye, someplace bright and sandy
like Afghanistan, or maybe Iraq.
But I didn't go. Because I didn't
consider it the right war. Or because
nobody made me.

PAUL: And are you hoping
I'll forgive you?

DAN: My point is maybe not
everyone's meant to be as courageous
as you are.

PAUL: It's not courage—

DAN: It's also
altruistic. Necessary. If you
don't do what you do then none of us will
ever have any idea what's really
going on.

PAUL: When I started out it was
all for self-esteem. I'm sure you started
out the same way too. I wanted people

to say I was brave, and heroic. Then
I began to hate it but I needed
that fix of adrenalin. The third stage,
where I am now? I don't really need it
anymore. But now I see the lies, now
I see how the people doing my job
don't get it. Or if they get it they don't
talk about it. They want success, they want
a seat at the Sunday morning talk show
round table. They want their own cable show.
I just want to chip away at those lies
now. But that's a losing game. Most people
don't care what's going on, or they don't know
what they're supposed to do. So we just stop
listening to the litany of evidence
of the coups we're pulling off, the phosphorus
bombs dropping on Fallujah in '04
that melted the skin off children—I could
go on and on and on and on. That's why
I object to the word altruistic.

DAN: Why? Because you're too angry?

PAUL: I see it
as a labyrinth: if you can find the truth
you get out. But you don't, it just gets worse,
you get more lost. And the harder you try
the darker it gets. As opposed to what,
being like you, I guess. Right, Dan? Who cares?
Let's watch some more TV. Let's drink more wine.
As long as I'm safe I don't need to do
a thing!

DAN: I guess that's fair.

PAUL: Sorry. See? This
is why I don't like to talk to people
besides my wife. People ask me questions
they don't want the answers to.

DAN: Do you want
to unmute the movie?

JACK: Morning, Paul. Dan,
the next time you come up here from LA
you bring me back a black twenty-year-old
girl. Okay?   *Light: dim sunrise.*

DAN: Next morning Jack says maybe
we'll go out on the land. Till an elder
stands up and peers out the kitchen window
at the snowflakes floating in a milky

morning light.

JACK: Elder says,

ELDER: Earth is moving
faster now.

JACK: He means this weather's messed up
cause of climate change. Says we'd better wait
until tomorrow.   *Moving image: blizzard*

DAN: The snow is moving   *in the window.*
faster now, I can't tell if it's falling
out of the sky or up from the treeless
lunarscape. —Jack, do you happen to know
any shamans around here?

PAUL: Dan's thinking
it'll make a good story.

DAN: It might be,
I don't know, entertaining.

JACK: A shaman?

DAN: You know, a medicine man. A healer
of some kind?

JACK: Sure. Roger.

DAN: Roger?

JACK: Roger
Umtoq. He's a storyteller? Makes stone
sculptures, junk like that. He lives out beyond
the trap lines in Minto Inlet. Don't know
if he's still alive.

DAN: Could you ask around
for his number? or email?

PAUL: Jack told me   *Light: evening.*
last winter one of these blizzards lasted
fourteen days.   *Moving image: blizzard*
                                                             in the window.
DAN: Fourteen days!

PAUL: That's a fortnight
to Canadians.

DAN: Later that evening
we're getting into bed, snow is whispering
beneath the windowpanes.

PAUL: I wouldn't mind
staying here for a while. Just between me
and you, my confessor. They're refusing
to send me anywhere interesting
anymore. I don't know why.

DAN: Are you scared
you'll be fired?

PAUL: Of course. Nobody's reading

anything anymore. Are you?

DAN: Reading
newspapers?

PAUL: And nobody's clicking on
these Arctic pieces either. My expense
reports are obscene.

DAN: Why not do something
else then?

PAUL: Like what? Maybe I could become
a wedding photographer.

DAN: Why don't you
write a book?

PAUL: I already wrote a book.
Remember? I think I sold like maybe
six copies in the US. One review
on Amazon said:

AMAZON: The lesson we learn,
that war lives in all of us, is neither
original nor particularly
helpful.

AMAZON: Author Watson is at his best
whilst giving us the sights and sounds of war,

AMAZON: but his memoir suffers when he aspires
to some kind of poetry whose only
loyalty is to the truth.

PAUL: I'm paraphrasing
now, of course, but what kind of an ass-jag   *Light: lights out.*
uses the word whilst?

DAN: Your book had no point
for me actually. To be completely   *Sound: wind howling.*
honest with you. I would read a chapter
or two, then have to put it down. And go
wash my hands. Because—it was all too much!
And repetitive. All these horrible
things you've lived through, I still don't understand
how you don't just surrender to profound
despair.

PAUL: Have I ever told you about
the time I met Mother Theresa?

DAN: No.

PAUL: I was stuck in Calcutta—

DAN: I'm going to
record this, okay?

PAUL: So I went over
to Mother's House. Which was this heavily

trafficked place, full of these shady-looking
characters wearing Rolex watches and
Italian business suits. There was a chair
by the door, and a sister said:

SISTER: Sit down,
and if she's willing she will come.

PAUL: Maybe
two or three days passed like this, till someone,
some sister comes downstairs and says,

SISTER: Mother
will see you now.

SISTER: Only for a short while,

SISTER: a moment if you're lucky.

PAUL: I turn on
my tape recorder and race up the stairs
where she's hobbling around in her knobby
crippled kind of bare feet in this small room
of hers with no doors,

PAUL: just some curtains and
I'm watching her shuffle back and forth from

PAUL: one doorway to the other,

PAUL: appearing
and then disappearing in the sunlight
and then shade.

PAUL: Never once looking at me.
Because I'd been to her treatment centers,
she didn't call them that, they're basically
places to go and die, right?

DAN: Right.

PAUL: Full of
row upon row of starving AIDS victims
and others,

PAUL: lying on these sorts of cots
very low to the ground.

PAUL: And they don't get
a lot of medical care, they get cleaned
and they get fed.

PAUL: They don't get fed a lot.

PAUL: And I was trying to be this heavy
on Mother Theresa, you know, saying,
Don't you think you should feed them some more food?

PAUL: Don't you think maybe you should be doing
this or that?

PAUL: And she said, They don't need food.
They need love. And she kept on saying that.

MOTHER: They need love. They need love. That's all. That's all.

PAUL: I was thinking, Wow, this is like shooting
ducks in a pond! This woman's a moron,
right?

DAN: Ha ha ha, right!

PAUL: So I go and write
my hit-piece about Mother Theresa.
It wasn't this blatant, but basically
what I said was that she was this harpy,
this, you know, cold-hearted nun mistreating
all these poor people. Well—bullshit. She's right.
What they *did* need was love. Because it was
respect. Either they die in the street or
they die in Mother's House. And if you die
in Mother's arms then at least you've died with
somebody loving you. And not because
they owe it to you, or because they feel
some familial obligation—they're just
doing it because they know you deserve
to be loved. You know? Maybe I'm a fool
but I think that was the point of my book
that no one bought.

DAN: So what you're saying is
war would disappear if we could all just
hold each others' hands?

PAUL: Why are you trying
to turn me into some kind of guru?

DAN: Am I?

PAUL: Like I've got some kind of answer
for you.

DAN: I don't know.

PAUL: That thing you wrote me
about your family, Dan. They disowned you
for no reason.

DAN: Right.

PAUL: And how your father
kept saying, There are things you do not know!
And how you look just like your dad's brother,
I keep thinking about that.

DAN: I do too.

PAUL: Did your father mean he's not your father?

DAN: I don't know. It's crazy, but—

PAUL: Why don't you
start asking some questions? That's what I'd do
if I were you.

DAN: Paul's laptop starts ringing.

PAUL: It's Skype. It's my wife. Stay here.

DAN: No I'll go
sit in the kitchen.

PAUL: No stay here. Hello?
Sweetness?

DAN: I hear Paul's wife's voice. I don't look
at the screen. I go out to the hallway
and sit by the pay phone. And try calling
home on an empty calling card.

PAUL: Sweetness,
I miss you so badly.

DAN: The next morning   *Light: dawn, no storm.*
things look different.

JACK: Next time you come up here,
Dan, you bring me back a bag of cocaine
and an AK-47.

DAN: We step
outside.

DAN: Snow snow.

DAN: Jerry's down on the ice
with his sled and his dog team. The sky is
bright, snow's drifting like pollen.

PAUL: Would you mind
riding with Jerry, Dan? Jack can pull me
behind his skidoo and I can shoot you
and the dogs that way.

DAN: Jerry's middle-aged
and mildly hunchbacked. I think I can see
that titanium plate in his forehead.

JERRY: Guys!
Guys! We're losing our sunlight here!

DAN: I snap
some pictures before my camera's frozen.

PAUL: Put it inside your coat! Put it next to
your skin!

DAN: I can't hear you!

JERRY: Hoot, hoot!

DAN: Jerry's   *Moving image, no sound:*
beating his dogs' muzzles with a short stick.   *Dan's footage of the dogs.*

JERRY: No, Ghost! Bad Ghost!

DAN: You call your dog Ghost? Why?

JERRY: I'm training him to lead. I had to sell
my old leader. But Ghost's a real scaredy
-cat.

DAN: The dogs are tangled in harnesses
                of yellow nylon cords.
JERRY: Misty wants to
                lead instead.
DAN: Who's Misty?
JERRY: The one in back.
DAN: She's cute. Smelly. Hyper. A bit dangerous.
JERRY: Real bitch.
DAN: They can't stop barking.
JERRY: Hoot! Hoot!
DAN: High
                -pitched yelps. They seem insane. Like a savage
                race of idiot wolves.
JERRY: Hoot! Hoot!
DAN: I'm missing
                my dog now. She's a miniature schnauzer
                these huskies would eat for breakfast. A few
                of them are eating their own shit. Tearing
                at hunks of meat.
JERRY: Hoot! Hoot, hoot!
DAN: Who knows what
                Jerry's trying to say?
JERRY: Sit your ass down,
                Dan! —Hoot, hoot, hoot!
DAN: And we're off. I'm sitting
                down, on my ass, on a blue plastic tarp
                with my rubber boots splayed in front, inches
                above the ice above the sea—
JERRY: Hold on
                to these ropes down here, Dan!
DAN: Jerry's kneeling
                behind my ear.
JERRY: Gee! Gee! Zaw!
DAN: Gee means right,
                I think. I've heard mushers say Haw! for left
                but Jerry says
JERRY: Zaw! —Hoot!
DAN: means faster. Paul's
                riding in a box on skis.
DAN: Jack's pulling
                him with his skidoo.
DAN: Red taillights dancing
                in a whorl of snow.
JERRY: Hoot, hoot!
DAN: You feel it

in your spine, your neck, your skull. The grinding
of the rusted runners on ice crystals
like sand.

Moving image, silent:
this dog sled ride,
Dan's POV.

DAN: Snow snow snow snow snow snow.

DAN: Cresting
another invisible ridge, the dogs
fan out to shit in streaks.

JERRY: Misty, no! Gee!
Gee!

DAN: We're moving onto the Arctic Sea,
and if we could only change direction
and head that way—

JERRY: Zaw! Zaw! Zaw!

DAN: If we could
only get the dogs to turn to the left
instead,

DAN: we'd be in Minto Inlet.

DAN: Where
Roger Umtoq the shaman lives.

JERRY   Misty,
no! —Zaw!

DAN: We stop at the floe's edge. The sea
is an undulating eternity
of black slush a few feet away. Seal heads
breaking through the new ice, their spectral eyes
on us.

PAUL: My feet are completely numb, Dan.

DAN: I think I bruised my tailbone.

JERRY: Hey guys! Guys!
These dogs aren't tired enough yet! Got to
keep going!

More footage, no
sound: dogs barking
in harness on the ice.

DAN: The dogs keep barking,

DAN: while Paul
sets up his tripod and shoots Jack kneeling
at the waterline,

DAN: tossing a snowball
onto the thin veneer of ice forming
on the water. It sounds like a pebble
bouncing off glass.

PAUL: Have you ever seen it
this melted before?

JACK: Usually ice floes
come down from the hill, usually springtime
like April May June?

JERRY: Hey guys! Guys! These dogs

are real worked up! Going to have to run them
some more!

JACK: Because that's when we get the winds?
But I've never seen it this warm before
in wintertime.

JERRY: Hey Dan.

DAN: Yeah.

JERRY: Put your weight
on this anchor.

DAN: What for?

JERRY: Just stand on this
and don't go anywhere. I need to go
drain my dragon.

DAN: The anchor's a steel claw
dug in the ice. Tied with a yellow cord
that's tied to the very last barking dog
in the team. Named Misty.

JERRY: Misty! shut up!

DAN: Jerry!

JERRY: Huh?

DAN: Do you know Roger Umtoq
the shaman in Minto Inlet?

JERRY: Old guy?
Told kids bullshit stories?

DAN: He's a healer
too.

JERRY: I don't know nothing about all that.

DAN: Can you take us out to Minto Inlet
to see him? Of course we'll pay you something,
Jerry.

JERRY: I'd like to take you to Minto
but the Roger I know out in Minto
died of heart attack last winter—

DAN: Misty
takes off,

JERRY: Misty no!

DAN: pulling the whole team,

DAN: and the sled starts sliding sideways,

DAN: I start
laughing, like I'm embarrassed,

DAN: as my boot
slips off the anchor,

DAN: as the anchor slips
out of the ice—

JERRY: What are you doing, Dan!

DAN: Me?

JERRY: Ghost! Ghost!

DAN: And for an instant I see
the top of the world from above,

PAUL: Hey Dan,
are you okay?

DAN: as the steel anchor wraps
around my ankle and whips me up off
my feet,

PAUL: I'm so sorry.

DAN: and the seal heads   *Light: Arctic night.*
duck back under the new ice.

PAUL: I'm feeling
so guilty.

DAN: We're back in our hotel room
and I can't move.

PAUL: How's your head?

DAN: It's all right.

PAUL: Do you need any more ice?

DAN: It's my groin   *TV on, no sound:*
that's killing me.   *entertainment news.*

PAUL: We're out of wine. You sure
you didn't bring anything?

DAN: I forgot,
I told you. I'm sorry.

PAUL: —You should've seen
yourself, you were sideways! You were almost
inverted! I don't know how that happened,
the physics of it, I mean. You don't have
anything to drink? no vodka?

DAN: I wish
I had some right now.

PAUL: This reminds me of
Abdul Haq—you know who he is right?

DAN: No.

PAUL: He was this mujahedeen famous for
defeating the Soviets in the '80s
with the CIA's help, of course. After
9/11, I went to interview
him in Peshawar.

DAN: Pakistan?

PAUL: —Here here here
record this.

DAN: Okay.

PAUL: I mean this guy looked

                exactly like Rob Reiner with a tan!
                and a bright white shalwar kameez. He hugged
                me! without knowing me! He was limping
                around on his prosthetic foot. I'm sure
                that's why he liked me.
DAN: Why?
PAUL: He was going
                back to Kabul so that when the US
                invaded he'd be an alternative
                to the Taliban. I'm sure he wanted
                revenge also, cause Talibs killed his wife
                and son a few years before, or maybe
                it was ISI—
DAN: ISI is what
                again, Paul?
PAUL: I was eating and sleeping
                on the floor, outside Kabul. With dried blood
                in the corner, bullet holes in the wall.
                Bathing in a bucket, with one toilet
                all plugged up with shit. Everybody there
                had dysentery. And somebody asked me,
                Have you heard what happened to Abdul Haq?
                He came over the Khyber Pass last week
                with 25 men, and Taliban troops
                ambushed him. He hid all night in the rocks
                calling the CIA for air support
                but no one came. Taliban captured him
                the next morning and hanged him from a tree
                with a metal noose. Cut off his dick and
                stuffed it in his mouth. Shot up his body
                till he was just this hanging piece of meat.
                I'm sorry, Dan. Sorry. I don't know why
                I'm thinking of him now. I don't know why
                I'm crying either! Maybe it's just cause
                you got tangled up in all that cord?
DAN: Paul's
                staring straight ahead. He's not here. Paul's not   *Moving image: snow*
                here anymore. I get up, head spinning,   *falling.*
                groin aching.
PAUL: Sorry, Dan. Sorry.
DAN: I see
                who he is now, finally: sitting there
                in his socks, his filthy sweatshirt, his eyes
                are like looking down a well. His greasy
                hair's all messed up. He's my older brother

sitting at the kitchen table, the day
they brought him back home from the hospital.
I was standing in the doorway watching
him pretend to eat something. Nobody
was saying a word. I could have sat down
with him. I was scared I'd catch his disease.
I thought, Sadness is an illness you catch
if you aren't careful enough. I ran
outside to play with friends. Are you hungry,
Paul? They've left some dinner on the table
for us.

10: YELLOWKNIFE

PAUL: It's like this French bistro called *Le Frolic*
              I think? just down the hill from the hotel
              in Yellowknife.   *Google directions:*
DAN: That whole flight from Ulu   *Ulukhaktok to*
              Paul's pitching me a TV show about   *Kugluktuk, Kugluktuk*
              life in the Arctic: *to Yellowknife.*
PAUL: *Fawlty Towers* meets
              White Fang!
DAN: I'm not really writing TV
              shows, Paul.
PAUL: Then your wife, your wife could write it
              for you!
DAN: I'm worried about the play, how
              to end it.
PAUL: I'm not saying it's a good
              French bistro. It's decent. I had dinner
              here on my way up. I'll get a bottle
              of their finest Cabernet. Do you want
              some beer? vodka?
DAN: How'd you meet your wife, Paul?
PAUL: My wife?
DAN: You never mention her. Except
              to say that she's "changed your life"—
PAUL: I don't talk
              about her for a reason.
DAN: Is she why
              you're doing better?
PAUL: Am I?
DAN: I don't know

what I thought would happen up here. I'm not
saying I think I failed. Maybe I did,
maybe I failed to get a story, but
I don't know yet. Because in many ways
you're just as fucked up as I'd imagined—

PAUL: Thank you.

DAN: In other ways you seem better
than I could ever hope to be.

PAUL: You sound
kind of disappointed, Dan.

DAN: What happened
to the ghost of William David Cleveland?
I kept meaning to ask—

PAUL: What do you mean
what happened to him?

DAN: Are you still haunted
by him? Does he follow you? Is he here
with us now? Or was that all a story
to sell books.

PAUL: He's here. He's gotten quieter,
that's true. It could be the meds. I worry
about my son, cosmic retribution
of some kind. I don't think about myself
anymore.

DAN: When did that change?

PAUL: I don't know
exactly. I know you were hoping for
an epiphany or something. Maybe
an exorcism. I know you wanted
to visit a shaman and have my soul
cleansed—

DAN: And cleanse myself.

PAUL: That's not how it works.
You get used to it. It just turns slowly
into something else. It's like when I called
Cleveland's mother—

DAN: Right that's in your book—

PAUL: No
that's just book-bullshit. When I wrote that book
I didn't understand it. I didn't
understand the conversation. You should
hear it sometime, remind me to send it
to you when I get home.

DAN: You recorded
the phone call?

PAUL:	That's right.
DAN:	Why?
PAUL:	Flew to Phoenix,
	rented a car. At the Ramada Inn
	turned on the AC
PAUL:	and pulled the blinds down	*Sound: answering*
	and picked up the phone:	*machine beeping.*
PAUL:	Um yes hello ma'am
	my name's Paul Watson. This is difficult
	for me to say. But I took that picture
	of your son that day in Mogadishu.
	I've wanted to meet you for years, to speak
	to you about what happened. And I hope
	you might be willing to give me some time
	in the next couple of days—
PAUL:	Had some dinner
	at the mall, back in the room the phone was—
PAUL:	Hello?
BROTHER:	This is William David Cleveland's
	brother.
PAUL:	Oh. —Hi, sir.
BROTHER:	Hi. Can I ask you
	never to call my mom again? She called
	me crying her eyes out cause you threw her
	into a really bad relapse.
PAUL:	Well, sir,
	it's just that I've been living with this thing
	for more than a decade now—
BROTHER:	You're talking
	about that picture you took of my brother
	drug through the streets?
PAUL:	That's right. And I'm hoping
	if I can understand my place in time
	and his place in time, then maybe we could
	bury a few things.
BROTHER:	Well, he was no different
	than all the people over there right now
	in Iraq and Afghanistan. Fighting
	for something they believe in, even when
	nobody else does.
PAUL:	That doesn't help me
	understand him as a person.
BROTHER:	That's him,
	that's him as a person.
PAUL:	I know him, sir,

only from that moment. And for my own
mental health—
BROTHER: He was a kind of weird kid
who didn't match in with nobody. But
he always knew he wanted to protect
people.
PAUL: Was your father in the navy,
sir?
BROTHER: He was an engine mechanic.
PAUL: And
did your brother have a wife?
BROTHER: Well he had
a couple of them.
PAUL: And you wouldn't know how
I might go about trying to track down
these women? Or other relatives?
BROTHER: Nope.
PAUL: He had some kids I understand.
BROTHER: Sorry?
PAUL: He had a few kids.
BROTHER: —Now are you looking
to do some kind of story again?
PAUL: Sir,
I just wish we could meet—
BROTHER: I don't care to
meet you at all.
PAUL: Do you hate me, sir?
BROTHER: What?
PAUL: You hate me, sir, I know it!
BROTHER: I don't hate
nobody, man!
PAUL: But—but I dishonored
your brother, that's what haunts me—
BROTHER: His honor
wasn't tarnished in the least.
PAUL: Well, sir, see
there's a lot of people who would argue
with you on that point.
BROTHER: They must not've been
one of the 3,000 people crowding
into a church that could hold only like
a hundred for his funeral. Must not've
been one of the 32 cars following
us all the way to the cemetery,
or the four helicopters with gunships

giving him an escort all the way. They
didn't feel he'd been dishonored.

PAUL: Others
who know him from my picture—

BROTHER: I don't care
about your picture! I'm not interested
in discussing it, I'm not interested
in meeting you, and I do apologize
if that offends you, sir—

PAUL: Could we do this
over email, sir?

BROTHER: No.

PAUL: Can't we just meet,
and you can see who I am—!

BROTHER: Once again
negative.

PAUL: Sir I have begged, I, I, I
don't understand why—

BROTHER: You're going to have to
deal with this on your own time.

PAUL: Your mother
hates me, sir. I read this interview about
that thing in Fallujah where they strung up
the American contractors from that bridge?
And your mother broke down crying and told
the reporter she hated the person
who did it then, like she hates the people
who do it now.

BROTHER: She was talking about
the people desecrating all of them
bodies.

PAUL: —No, sir, she was talking about
me, sir! I know it!

BROTHER: The thing of it was,
when David got shot down and went missing?
since our mom had remarried and taken
a different name, they told his stepmother
he'd been killed in action. We found out while
watching Peter Jennings. When my mother
recognized David's feet. Cause they looked like
his dad's. If it weren't for your picture
we might've never found out.

PAUL: You must blame
me for that much, sir—

BROTHER: Man, you don't listen

very well, do you?

PAUL: Do you want to know
why I did it?

BROTHER: No.

PAUL: Why not?

BROTHER: Explaining
don't change the fact a thing got done.

PAUL: A week
before, another Black Hawk got shot down,
and kids were parading the body parts
of servicemen through the streets like pennants
at a baseball game. And the Pentagon
denied it. They said it didn't happen.
Because I didn't have a picture.

BROTHER: Right.

PAUL: I wasn't a machine, I cared.

BROTHER: Right.

PAUL: And
honestly, sir, I believe your brother
would still be alive today if people
had known the truth.

BROTHER: From my own life I'd say,
and I was in the Air Force for ten years,
I volunteered to go to Somalia
but they wouldn't let me go, cause of work,
where I was. But I can honestly say
I'd have no problem if I'd been the one
in my brother's shoes.

PAUL: You would've wanted
that picture taken?

BROTHER: I would've.

PAUL: Why, sir?
for the reason I just explained or?

BROTHER: Both,
for the reason you just said and because
you're just doing your job.

PAUL: Well I'm grateful
to you for saying that.

BROTHER: Not a problem.

PAUL: It takes a large weight off. I only wish
the rest of your family felt the same way.

BROTHER: You're going to have to take my word on that
unfortunately.

PAUL: Oh yeah no, I won't go
down that route, sir.

BROTHER: I appreciate that, sir.

PAUL: I'm just talking about the larger world here.

BROTHER: Well the world's fucked up.

PAUL: Sure.

BROTHER: Short and sweet, the world's a fallen place. Ha ha ha.

PAUL: And I hope this won't upset you but one thing that still haunts me is that I heard a voice when I took that picture. And your brother warned me: If you do this I will own you forever.

BROTHER: Well how do you know David meant something bad?

PAUL: He said I will own you forever—

BROTHER: Maybe he meant you owe him something now.

PAUL: Like what?

BROTHER: Look, I've got to go pick up my boy.

PAUL: Okay sir, I forgot to ask you your name.

BROTHER: Ray.

PAUL: Ray, that's my dad's name.

RAY: Ha ha ha.

PAUL: Sir, please apologize to your mother for me?

RAY: Good night.

PAUL: Good night.

DAN: The phone's hung up. The hum fades out.

DAN: Footsteps on hotel carpeting. The zipping up of a bag.

DAN: After dinner we're struggling through blistering wind,

DAN: sand snow,

DAN: to the Hotel Explorer, this strangely lavish, somewhat Soviet, high-rise hotel for diplomats from the south.

PAUL: I'm going up to Resolute soon. Where the American scientists hang out all summer long.

DAN: —I can't hear you!

PAUL: I said
I'm doing a story about robot
submarines!

DAN: That's awesome! Maybe I'll try
for a grant to go with you!

PAUL: Great!

DAN: We step
inside the elevator.

PAUL: I'm leaving
first thing in the morning. Fuck me.

DAN: My flight's
in the afternoon. So I guess this is
goodbye.

PAUL: Here's my floor. So.

DAN: Hey Paul, thank you
for writing back to me for years now. And
for writing back in the first place. It's hard
to explain everything it's meant to me,
to be able to leave my home and go
someplace like this, with somebody like you,
even for a short while.

DAN: But I don't say
any of that. I say:

DAN: Paul, I don't know
if this play's going to be any good. But
I'll email it to you when I'm done.

PAUL: Don't
bother, I won't read it. I can't look back
on all this old stuff anymore, Dan. But
I'm happy you're the one writing it. Bye
now. Safe flight.

DAN: The elevator closes   *Moving image: snow*
and I wonder if I'll ever see him   *falling.*
again.

PAUL: My deepest apologies, Dan,
for not writing sooner. I'm in Resolute
where I've just destroyed all my computer
equipment, by accident, by dropping
my bag off the side of an icebreaker.   *Google terrain: Resolute.*
I simply lost my grip! as we broke through
miles and miles of ice near Taloyoak.

DAN: I'm working on our play at a theater
in Minneapolis, in a neighborhood

called Little Mogadishu. Somali
refugees everywhere. Girls in hijabs
walking down the sidewalk. It would be strange
to have you with me here, Paul. I don't know
whether you'd hate it. Or love it.

PAUL: Dear Dan,
just between me and you, my confessor:
the big news is I'm back in Kandahar.
It's summer again and the Taliban's
itching for a fight. The *Toronto Star*
wants its pretty thin coverage here beefed up,
and if I want to keep my wife and son
in new snow boots I need to make myself
valuable to the *Star*. And Canada's
responsible for Kandahar. Truth is
I'm no different than all those Americans
driving their trucks in near suicidal
conditions in Iraq, just to pay off
mortgages in Florida. This is what
I've come to: I'm a mercenary and
a desperate one at that. Just between me
and my confessor. But there's something else:
I feel like Cleveland's happy I've come back,
though I don't know why yet. Maybe you'll come
visit me sometime? Someplace relaxing
like Kabul. Maybe there's a book in it,
or a play. So what do you say? Will you
come, Dan? I promise I'll keep you as safe
as I can. Though of course nobody knows
what can happen out here. Talk to you soon,
your friend Paul.

Google map:
Minneapolis.

Google Earth:
Kandahar.

Google Earth:
Kabul.

END OF PLAY

THE HOUSE IN SCARSDALE

a memoir for the stage

The House in Scarsdale: A Memoir for the Stage was winner of the PEN America Award for Drama, runner-up for the Humanitas/Center Theatre Group Playwriting Prize, shortlisted for an LA Drama Critics Circle Award for Writing, and benefited from the Center Theatre Group Writers' Workshop, residencies at the New Harmony Project and the Rockefeller Foundation's Bellagio Center in Bellagio, Italy, and readings and workshops at Atlantic Theater Company, Center Theatre Group, Hartford Stage, Play-PerView, and PTP/NYC.

The House in Scarsdale: A Memoir for the Stage was excerpted in the *Hopkins Review* (Vol. 8, No. 2) and the *New England Review* (Vol. 38, No. 3).

The world premiere of *The House in Scarsdale: A Memoir for the Stage* was produced in 2017 by The Theatre @ Boston Court in Pasadena, California, Co-Artistic Directors Jessica Kubzanksy and Michael Michetti.

Cast
DAN: Tim Cummings
DAN: Brian Henderson

Creative Team
Director: Michael Michetti
Scenic: Sara Ryung Clement
Costume: Kate Bergh
Lighting: Elizabeth Harper
Projection: Tom Ontiveros
Sound: John Nobori
Assistant Director: Ashley Steed
Dramaturg: Emilie Beck
Production Stage Manager: Alyssa Escalante
Photography: Ed Krieger

Characters:
Two play all the roles—an actor in their 30s, who plays Dan most of the time, and an actor in their 50s to play the "other" Dan and most every other character.

The younger actor has the first line of the play and with each new character heading—even when it's the same character—the actors alternate.

Place & Time:
Various.

Notes:
The right-hand column of the script contains suggestions of photographs, video, maps, etc., to be projected somewhere prominent onstage, as well as suggestions of light and sound.

The perforated lines in scene five are meant to suggest seamless yet significant changes in setting.

Running time is 90-100 minutes without an intermission.

For my brother

Come back, come back, my wretched, feeble and unwanted child.

—John Cheever

1: WHAT HAS HE GIVEN YOU?

DAN: The first thing I remember is looking *A dark place.*
up at his face.

DAN: Sunlight in the window,

DAN: I'm playing on the floor.

DAN: The whole family's
sleeping still.

DAN: My father's younger brother
is sitting beside the window looking
down at me. *A window*

DAN: Smiling. With a long black beard *appears.*
and heavy, black-framed glasses, he looks like
a hobo, and a poet.

DAN: He gives me
a children's Bible.

DAN: No he's giving you
something else,

DAN: some other kind of gift. —What's
he giving me?

DAN: What has he given you

DAN: —before he walks out the door?

Overcast

2: THINGS YOU DO NOT KNOW
light,

SKIP: Hey!

DAN: Hey! *July,*

SKIP: How are you?

DAN: —How are *you?* *New Jersey.*

SKIP: So good
to see you!

DAN: Good to see *you!* You look great.

SKIP: Yeah right.

DAN: You *do!*

SKIP: You look the same. Except
you're about ten feet taller—Danny!

DAN: —Skip,
thanks for answering that message I sent you.

SKIP: Isn't Facebook amazing?

DAN: All I did
was type your name and there you were—!

SKIP: Too bad
I couldn't get here sooner, otherwise
we could've hung out!

DAN: Well it's not your fault
I've got rehearsal.

SKIP: Oh yeah?

DAN: For a play.

SKIP: That's amazing! You're an actor?

DAN: I write
plays and uh, poems.

SKIP: Ha ha ha! —So how long
do you think it'll take to get into
the city?

DAN: Don't know, half an hour?

SKIP: Sorry
about the mess, been driving cross-country,   *They're sitting*
the kids are with their mom on Long Island   *in a car but*
and I have to pick them up and take them
to Vermont for summer camp and then how   *please don't pretend*
the hell do we get out of here?   *to drive.*

DAN: Go left
at this sign.

SKIP: Right here?

DAN: Go straight and then—

SKIP: God
New Jersey's so confusing! Even worse
than like Marin!

DAN: Is that where you live, Skip,
in Marin?

SKIP: San Francisco, but I lived
in Marin for about a year after
the divorce.

DAN: Oh. Right. Sorry.

SKIP: So tell me
how long's it been?

DAN: I don't know, like almost
twenty years?

SKIP: Are you married?

DAN: Our wedding
was four years ago, we've lived in LA
three years now, no kids and we're coming up
on a right at this light not a sharp right

more like—

SKIP: One of those soft sort of bear-right
kind of rights—

DAN: Right, and then we take our lives
in our hands—

SKIP: Right right!

DAN: In classic Jersey
style—

SKIP: That's hilarious! Your wife's an actress
I heard? —That's amazing!

DAN: She grew up here,
I'm staying with her folks to save money
while I'm rehearsing this play—

SKIP: Which way now?
Left?

DAN: Right. —No I meant right, left.

SKIP: —Ha ha ha!

DAN: Know what? Why don't we just type it in   *Map: Garden State*
the Garmin. —Don't want to drive to Scarsdale   *Parkway. Somewhere*
by mistake!   *around Exit 140*

SKIP: Is that where your parents live   *maybe.*
still, in Scarsdale?

DAN: They moved eight years ago   *We'll follow*
to Virginia.   *their progress*

SKIP: But everybody's still   *into Manhattan*
alive? their health's good?

DAN: I have no idea.   *on a projection screen*

SKIP: What do you mean?   *like a GPS*

DAN: They stopped talking to me   *but weirder,*
about five years ago, and I don't know
why.   *interspersed*

SKIP: Oh right well families can be tough.   *here and there*

DAN: But   *with pictures, video*
it's a bit weirder than that, cause I mean
they didn't speak to my sister for years,   *of the landscape*
they didn't speak to Paul. They hardly speak   *perhaps,*
to my other brothers. Cause they have this
tendency toward paranoia—well   *perhaps*
you know, right?   *of Dan and Skip's*

SKIP: You know, what little I know   *family.*
about Jimmy your mother's brother—?

DAN: Right.

SKIP: Is that there's some kind of genetic thing
going on.   *We're in Dan's*

DAN: I've always wondered about   *head,*

Jimmy, what was wrong with—

SKIP: He's a schizo.   *essentially.*

DAN: Oh. Okay.

SKIP: And from what I understand
it's like, it skips? it's hereditary
so you'd better watch your back ha ha ha!

DAN: There's a lot of truth to that. My parents
are pretty messed up. Like I said. Cause like
they never had any friends. They rarely
left the house. They suffer from depression
and anxiety, though they don't believe
in psychology. —But lately I feel
there's something else happening here, something
they don't want me to find out.

SKIP: Like what?

DAN: Well,
for instance my mother never told me
what you just told me, that her brother was
schizophrenic.

SKIP: Ha ha ha.

DAN: Now maybe
she didn't know—

SKIP: I think everybody's
always been pretty aware what was wrong
with Jimmy. Like did you hear how he tried
to torch your grandparents' house, that mansion
in Scarsdale? what's it called?

DAN: Old Ridge.

SKIP: Old Ridge,
right.

DAN: I found something in the *New York Times*
when the house was sold: a million dollars
in 1962. With thirty rooms
on seven acres. On the highest hill
in Westchester County, it said. With views
of the Long Island Sound—

SKIP: That place was like
Fall of the House of Usher!

DAN: Ha ha ha.

SKIP: And then they had to ship Jimmy away
to Canada, where they paid some Christians
to take care of him. And this quack doctor
who'd shoot him full of vitamin B6
or something, which didn't make Jimmy sane.

DAN: Is he still alive?

SKIP: I have no idea!
    Cause as you know your mother's mother was
    a raging alcoholic.
DAN: I've heard that.
SKIP: Like off the charts. I think it's safe to say
    the drinking screwed them all up. Alcohol
    has a lot to do with the way children
    form themselves. Right?
DAN: Right.
SKIP: Like I think I heard
    your grandmother used to lock your mother
    in the closet with a glass of water
    overnight? Ever hear that?
DAN: Not that one
    but others. Like how her mother got drunk
    and one day tried to slip out of the house
    naked—
SKIP: Right right!—except for like a mink
    over her panties—
DAN: And my mother blocked
    the front door, so her mother beat her up,
    scratched her and kicked her. So that by the time
    Grandpa came home from work in the city
    and found his daughter asleep on the floor
    in front of the door, and his wife passed out
    on the couch mostly naked—well he knew
    he could divorce her and keep custody
    of the girls. His girls. Which was a rare thing
    in those days.
SKIP: Still is.
DAN: I'll bet.
SKIP: —All I know
    is your grandfather was a legend.
DAN: Right,
    my mother was always saying—
SKIP: He was
    a business genius but at the same time
    just like this Joe Blow who'd eat a hot dog
    with you out on Broadway. Then back inside
    he's chewing your head off! —I mean the love
    and respect for him was hard to believe.
DAN: Sounds like it.
SKIP: I consider myself blessed
    to have had him as a stepfather. Blessed.
    He lost his father too. And his mother.

DAN: I know.
SKIP: Eight years old and he's an orphan
           in Hoboken. Like Dickens or something.
           Dies with offices in Times Square, sweatshops
           in China. If you bought a business shirt
           in like the sixties, seventies, eighties
           at a Kmart or Walmart, two of his
           big deals, what you were really buying was
           your grandfather's shirt.
DAN: My mother would say
           he was kind of obsessive-compulsive
           about work.
SKIP: Of course he was! But that's why
           he succeeded! —God those OCD guys
           make so much money.
DAN: Ha ha ha.
SKIP: I know
           your grandmother fought him on that, his work,
           during the divorce. Which was a shitshow
           by the way. In the papers. With rumors
           of affairs in places like Jamaica
           with celebrities like Kirk Douglas—real
           kinky stuff!
DAN: Was she an alcoholic
           cause her son went insane and her husband
           was a workaholic?
SKIP: That's an idea.
           But this was before I was on the scene,
           Danny. I was just a kid when my mom
           met your grandfather. He'd sold that mansion
           in Scarsdale, your grandmother hightailed it
           to Florida to shack up with some guy
           everybody called the diabetic
           gigolo—
DAN: Ha ha ha.
SKIP: —Oh yeah it's just
           like this classic scenario: you're forty,
           back on the market, but you look around
           and there's nothing but a bunch of divorced
           losers like you!
DAN: Right right.
SKIP: After a while
           you get jaded. Cause the women these days
           don't have that much to talk about.
DAN: They don't?

SKIP:	And the older gals in San Francisco,
	let us just say they have these er, ideas
	that are more progressive than mine.
DAN:	Right right.
SKIP:	When they climb into my black Escalade
	they're like—What the *fuck?* You know?
DAN:	Ha ha ha.
SKIP:	Except pretty soon it's turning them on
	—It's so big! They're being bad! Their latest
	is that they don't watch TV, they listen
	to NPR.
DAN:	Right.
SKIP:	—I swear if I hear
	what I call the divorcée trifecta
	with the Terry Gross thing, she's got a cat
	and eats a raw diet—?
DAN:	Uh huh.
SKIP:	And then
	she's ordering a glass of *chardonnay?*
	—I'm so out of there.
DAN:	Ha ha ha.
SKIP:	My ex
	is bipolar. She used to drink a lot
	of wine.
DAN:	Sure.
SKIP:	Where were we? You were talking
	about *your* family.
DAN:	Oh well the problem
	began before our wedding. My mother
	would call and talk in this circular way
	about nothing, it's a clinical term
	called logorrhea and she has it and
	it's getting worse with age, and she'd just talk
	incessantly about how nobody
	was coming to our wedding—
SKIP:	Ha ha ha.
DAN:	Cause like I said they were estranged from Paul
	and Joyce. And my father hadn't talked to
	his brothers in decades. And my mother
	had no family left cause she sued you all
	over Grandpa's will—
SKIP:	Right right.
DAN:	And also
	they must've been feeling overwhelmed cause
	my brother was back in the hospital

	again.	
SKIP:	Which—?	
DAN:	I don't know how much you know already.	
SKIP:	—Nothing!	
DAN:	Well my brother Paul got depressed in high school—	
SKIP:	Well in those days we forget: people didn't like to talk about these things.	
DAN:	Right right.	
SKIP:	If you were nuts they'd give you like a lobotomy.	
DAN:	Right but this was the late-eighties. And it's true we didn't live on the Upper West Side, but my parents never even took Paul to see a therapist. Even after he tried to kill himself.	
SKIP:	What? how?	
DAN:	He jumped out of our attic window.	
SKIP:	Jesus Christ.	
DAN:	I was in the driveway and I saw him stumbling around the side of the house to the front door with his shoulders white with snow. The back of his head too. I can see him barefoot, though I don't really remember if he was or not. He was seventeen and I was twelve, and I'm sure it formed me as a writer ha ha ha.	*A patch* *of sun,*
SKIP:	—Right right right!	*then back*
DAN:	And that's why I wanted to see you, Skip. You always seemed so normal. And so cool, with your black Trans-Am and those leopard-print satin sheets on your water bed.	*to the clouds.*
SKIP:	—I mean if those sheets could talk—!	
DAN:	Cause like I emailed, I've been researching my family. Well, our family. For a play. Maybe a memoir, we'll see. Like it's a mystery, which it is to me. Just searching for a solution to, you know—What happened? Six grown children who hardly ever speak to each other,	

all of whom are mentally unstable,
in my opinion, like my brother Paul
who in addition to the depression
could probably be classified borderline
autistic. And I had like this breakdown
when my family disowned me or maybe
it's best to think of it as a pit stop
cause I tend to seem normal, I've been told
I *seem* normal. But it hasn't been good
for my marriage, my career, my liver
either, which I'm going to have to deal with
at some point. —So what was wrong with my folks,
Skip? Any ideas?

SKIP: Well you know I, I
was on the outside, in my position.

DAN: Sure.

SKIP: And when I'd come over it was fun.

DAN: —"Fun"?

SKIP: You know. Polite. There'd be all this food
and we'd all sit around talking. Just like
Leave It to Beaver.

DAN: That's impossible.
We never had fun. —Or food.

SKIP: And your dad
was such a smart guy. So smart. Still must be.

DAN: Why does everybody think that?

SKIP: He's not?

DAN: No, mostly he just watched TV and read
science-fiction and fantasy novels.
Westerns too. He never finished college.
Every time our mother made us show him
our report cards, he'd just shrug and mumble,
Better than I ever did.

SKIP: Well how much
can you really know about a family
you see like once a year.

DAN: Another thing
I'm trying to figure out is how much
did my grandfather help us with money?

SKIP: Money?

DAN: Yeah, cause my father never seemed
to be all that busy. He'd climb the stairs
to his so-called office in the attic
and act like a "computer consultant,"
whatever that was. I don't remember

his phone ringing much. And we lived without
health insurance—

SKIP: Well from what I know—
DAN: Right—
SKIP: From what I heard—there'd been these discussions
where my mother said to your grandfather,
We should help these kids out. You know? Send them
to college.
DAN: Oh. Okay.
SKIP: Other than that
I know nothing!
DAN: Huh.
SKIP: —But they were happy
to do it.
DAN: It's too bad it had to be
a secret though.
SKIP: See but the problem was
really your grandfather. Cause even I
run into this: he was so successful
that you're always kind of like—that's the bar?
and the odds of being that successful
are infinitesimal. It's a weight
to carry round, believe me.
DAN: What's your job,
Skip? I should've asked.
SKIP: I sell cooling fans
for high-tech? It doesn't get me laid but
I was in your grandfather's company
for many years—
DAN: Right right—
SKIP: And it was just
ugh.
DAN: For what reason?
SKIP: And then your cousin
Don came onboard. And he's president now.
Your cousin Mitchell has grown quite wealthy
in title insurance. So it's a tough,
tough business, the garment industry. Real
bottom feeders. —But that's a good topic
for a memoir maybe: how money tears
a family apart.   *Map: Route 1,*
DAN: How much is the toll?
SKIP: I got it.   *Pulaski Skyway,*
DAN: —Let me, Skip.   *Hoboken, NJ,*
SKIP: No be my guest,

asshole! —You can tell I'm from out of town, *heading into the*
letting people into my lane. —I'm not *Holland Tunnel.*
letting you in here! —Got the New Yorker
coming back in me!

DAN: Right right.
SKIP: —This is cash
-only, sugar tits!
DAN: Can I ask you, Skip?
before we run out of time. Overnight *Tunnel lighting.*
every aunt and uncle, every cousin
—everybody vanished.
SKIP: Right.
DAN: Did you feel
like my family just spiraled away or
was it more like my mother and father
destroyed everything?
SKIP: That was more the thing
of it, yeah.
DAN: Right. Right.
SKIP: —Cause we've never known.
I mean your mother was the closest thing
I had to a sister. And her sisters
were crushed by it. Just crushed! So—do you think
your father had an influence on what
she did?
DAN: Did my father—?
SKIP: Did he force her
to sue us all like that?
DAN: I don't think so.
Cause even though they always seemed to hate
each other, they also seemed perfectly
matched. You know?
SKIP: Did he ever beat her up?
or the kids?
DAN: I mean, sometimes he'd throw things
at us. Shoes. Or punch walls. He'd kick the dogs
and all our dogs went insane. He'd call us
fucking idiots. But most of the time
he just never spoke.
SKIP: So if I hear you
correctly: these lawsuits gave your parents
like this common enemy?
DAN: —Right!
SKIP: A cause,
like when some dictator in Africa

tells his country the neighboring country's
invading—

DAN: It's pathological too
in the sense that when they went after me
and my wife, that day we fell out with them?
—it was like they were turned on somehow.

SKIP: How?

DAN: It's like I'd never seen them so in love
before.

SKIP: But what was the fight about though?

DAN: I don't know. I don't know. I don't know how
to explain it. I wish I could just say
my father was a child molester or
my mother smoked crack. We were visiting
a month before our wedding. I had grown
a beard, and my hair was somewhat longer
but not like some hippie: like somebody
who drives a hybrid car and listens to
NPR.

SKIP: Ha ha ha.

DAN: Sitting outside   *Sunlight, May*
when my father asked me,

HAROLD: What's wrong with you?   *afternoon. Green.*

DAN: What?

HAROLD: What's wrong with you? There must be something
terribly wrong to make you look the way
you look.

DAN: How do I look—?

HAROLD: Like you're homeless.
Like you're schizophrenic.

DAN: What do you mean—?

HAROLD: You look just like my brother Brian.

DAN: So?

HAROLD: You're the spitting image of him. —Let's go
for a walk.

DAN: No.

HAROLD: Let's go for a walk.

DAN: Why?

HAROLD: There are things you do not know.

DAN: Then tell me.

HAROLD: —There are things you don't know!

DAN: I drove away   *Out of*
and I haven't heard from them since.

SKIP: So where   *the tunnel,*
should I drop you?

DAN: Oh. Well, I need to be   *clouds again.*
            downtown but wherever's good for you—

SKIP: Hey   *Map: downtown*
            I'm just driving you!   *Manhattan. Canal*

DAN: Union Square then. Thanks.   *Street.*

SKIP: I need to drive more aggressively here
            —is it the Gay Pride Parade today
            or what—?

DAN: So you never heard anything
            suspicious about my uncle?

SKIP: Your who—?

DAN: My father's younger brother Brian. Cause
            it would make so much sense. She's stuck at home
            with three kids already. With a husband
            she hates, who hates her. Whose younger brother
            is taller, smarter, funnier. Who lives
            in the neighborhood, with his mother but
            he's still young. And passionate. Protesting
            the bombing of Cambodia. Reading
            Marshall McLuhan, noodling his guitar,
            transcribing Neruda poems. All it takes
            is an afternoon.

SKIP: Sounds like you're talking
            to the wrong uncle here, Danny Boy!

DAN: Right.

SKIP: Ha ha ha.

DAN: Oh, I meant to ask you, Skip,
            is Regina—?

SKIP: Oh yeah she's still bopping
            around. You know, telling me what to do
            like—Get your pants pressed!

DAN: Do you think I could
            maybe call her sometime?

SKIP: My mom won't talk
            to you. Actually she told me not to
            pick you up today. She says we can't trust
            your family. But I said you're blood, sort of,
            and maybe we'll learn something.

DAN: What about
            my mother's sisters?

SKIP: That's another thing   *Map: Union Square.*
            I'm supposed to let you know: nobody's
            going to talk to you. And nobody's mad
            at you, Danny—

DAN: And I'm not mad at them—

SKIP: But you shouldn't contact us anymore.

DAN: Right.

SKIP: About this family stuff anyway,
            understand? Here's my card. —Listen, better   *Rain,*
            get going. We'll get together sometime
            on the other coast.   *a summer*

3: WHAT YOU FEEL IS TRUE   *thunderstorm.*

DAN: Waiting for the lights to change,   *Traffic,*

DAN: this rain is
            rancid. Trash is melting. And you're wondering, *brakes shrieking.*

DAN: —What are they afraid of?

DAN: In a black box   *Animation:.*
            on MacDougal Street, watching an actor
            tell a ghost story you wrote years ago   *black on white*
            when you still had a family,

DAN: I'm swiping   *line drawings*
            through Facebook on my phone until I find
            Aunt Darcy. My godmother.   *of something like*

DARCY: Dear Danny,
            how wonderful it is to hear from you   *all this.*
            after so long!

DAN: She looks like my mother
            but younger. And thinner. Blonde. A facelift,
            or more than one.

DARCY: I've often thought of you
            and your brothers and sisters and wondered
            how you'd turn out.

DAN: One son looks like the prince
            of the family, preppy. A younger son
            looks older, overweight and depressive
            after years of drug abuse. Two more sons
            I've never met. All arranged on a couch   *Drawing*
            with a bevy of Cavalier King Charles   *of this portrait*
            Spaniels in the Hamptons.   *comes together.*

DARCY: I remember
            so fondly driving to the Scarsdale pool
            to spend the afternoon with you. I've missed
            being a part of your lives!

DAN: In Newark   *Map: Newark*
            train station, almost midnight, I'm waiting   *Penn Train Station.*
            for the last connection.

DARCY: It's sad to read
          that you feel you were "basically disowned"
          by your parents. Have you ever asked why?
DAN: A colleague asked me in my rental car
          last month, we were teaching at a conference   *Map: Sewanee,*
          down south, as the walls of the Cumberland   *Tennessee.*
          Plateau rose around us,
SOUTHERNER: But do you *feel*
          like a New Yorker?
DAN: I do now. Listening   *Map: Newark.*
          to the people on the platform saying
          wonderful things like,
PERSON: Are you Hispanic
          or Latino?
PERSON: —It's the same thing!   *Line drawings*
PERSON: I thought
          you're from the Caribbean?   *forming*
PERSON: That's right but
          that's Latino.   *some version*
PERSON: —Oh!
DAN: This Italian guy's   *of this.*
          cradling his sleeping son while flirting with
          Asian twins:
GUY: Do you girls go all the way
          to Roselle?
DAN: I recognize in the rough
          way of walking and talking and thinking
          what I imagine my grandfather was
          and who I used to be.
DARCY: I'd be happy
          to speak with you, Danny. But I'm afraid
          I can't shed much light. There's been so much pain
          in our family. It's all so confusing!
          and the truth is I really don't know much
          anyway.
DAN: A guy on the platform, high
          or schizophrenic or both, keeps looking
          over his shoulder at me, now staggering
          my way—is that his dick?
DAN: —Is he going to   *Line drawings*
          throw up?
DAN: Does he have a handgun? He calls   *like a Rorschach,*
          out to me,
MAN: Hey man, next train every hour
          on the hour!

MAN: Hey man,
MAN: next hour every train
            on the brain!   *or a palimpsest*
DAN: And shuffling past a white cop
            he shuts his mouth.   *of everything.*
DARCY: But please do keep in touch
            with us, Danny. Maybe our paths will cross
            somewhere down the line?
DAN: Back home in LA   *Sun and shadows.*
            I make an appointment with a psychic
            named Eddie. He's flamboyant, he grew up
            in Appalachia. Think Liberace   *Water*
            meets *Deliverance.*   *trickling*
EDDIE: I'm feeling a feather,   *in a fountain.*
            does a feather mean anything to you?
DAN: No.   *New-age*
EDDIE: How bout a fountain?   *pan-flute music*
DAN: Um—   *low.*
EDDIE: My heavens
            —you ever see your grandma's ying-yang?
DAN: Her?
EDDIE: Hoo-ha. Coochie.
DAN: —Yes! —My father's mother,
            it's one of my only memories of her,
            when my older sister was helping her
            get dressed.
EDDIE: Isn't that unbelievable?
DAN: It is. He keeps talking. About Old Ridge,
            that haunted house where my mother grew up—
EDDIE: Oh God no.
DAN: What is it?
EDDIE: I feel incest
            everywhere.
DAN: Yeah.
EDDIE: Everywhere.
DAN: I ask him
            about my uncle Brian. —Could he be
            my father, Eddie?
EDDIE: I feel what you feel
            is true is true.
DAN: That's good.
EDDIE: Now I don't know
            whether it's Brian or somebody else—
DAN: Like who—?
EDDIE: Cause I'm hearing like a Mickey

or Mick—

DAN: But he tells me not to worry,
I'll find out the truth about my father
soon enough.

EDDIE: But in order to resolve   *Sunlight grows.*
this mystery, Dan, you must first lose yourself
in unfamiliar terrain. Make your life
a never-finished work of art. Live life
outside this bubble you've created here
in LA with your writing and running
and alcohol and internet porn. Say,
Higher Being, step into my body,
this prison of time, this suit of decay,
and help me to see Eddie's driveway full
of sunlight and roses and hummingbirds   *Brilliant sun.*
for what they truly are: vibrating light
that is love. And help me to remember
what is true. Spirit says we'd ask for that
every day. With intentions fast and pure
so you can write it all down. And that's how
we're going to build a bridge back to the truth
of who you are.

DAN: Thank you.

EDDIE: —And move your bed
away from the window. There's going to be
a big old earthquake next month.

DAN: I dig up
her number.

REGINA: Hello, Regina speaking.
I'm away from my phone, obviously
ha ha ha. Or I'm here and don't want to   *Slowly giving way to:*
talk to you, ha ha ha. But leave your name
and number—

DAN: I hang up. And as soon as
I find myself back in New York I drive   *autumn*
out to Rye. To this nineteenth-century
Italian-style villa. A polo field,
not one but two golf courses, a beach club
on the Sound. Tennis, squash. Where once we dressed
in blazers and ties and picked at our fish   *twilight.*
in the Biltmore Room. Crystal chandeliers,
tall candles flickering above snow-white
table cloths. I'm trembling as I reach out
to ring her bell—

                                        Ding.

4: YOUR FATHER'S A LOSER

REGINA: Do I know you?   *Video projection:*

DAN: I'm your grandson. Your uh,   *branches*
step-grandson.

REGINA: Danny?   *of orange*

DAN: Dan. Can I come in?   *oak leaves*

REGINA: Well you're here, aren't you.

DAN: Thanks.   *in a stately window*

REGINA: So you live   *in Westchester, NY.*
in Hollywood now?

DAN: Nearby. My wife is
an actor.

REGINA: And you, are you successful?

DAN: I hope so.

REGINA: Any kids?   *Just some chairs*

DAN: Not yet. Maybe   *maybe.*
one day.

REGINA: You're old. You look like you could use
a shave. How'd you find me?

DAN: I remembered
how you, Grandpa and Skip used to live here
at the country club—

REGINA: I mean who let you
past the gate?

DAN: I said I was your grandson
and wanted to surprise you.

REGINA: You're lucky
you rang my bell tonight, I'm leaving for
Florida first thing—

DAN: And I'm well aware
you don't want to talk to me—

REGINA: So tell me,
your brother threw himself out the window?

DAN: Yeah—in a nutshell—

REGINA: Can you make this box   *No props*
stand up for me please?   *or miming*

DAN: He got depressed and—   *please.*

REGINA: Well it's the first I've heard of such a thing!
All we ever knew was Paul was gone and
nobody ever said if he moved out
or got thrown out—

DAN: He got thrown out. He lived
at home for a while, after he flunked out
of college.

REGINA: —Well they should've done something
                    about it! You don't give up on family.
DAN: I know.
REGINA: And he's not married? Is he a gay?
                    Cause gay is very popular these days.
DAN: I don't know. Maybe.
REGINA: And where's he live now?
DAN: Scarsdale. Never left. He's the computer
                    tech guy at the town hall.
REGINA: Well he must be
                    very lonely. And how old are you now,
                    Danny?
DAN: Thirty-six. No, thirty-seven
                    last week. Jesus.
REGINA: It's unbelievable,
                    this life! Isn't it? So fast.
DAN: You look good.
                    You seem exactly the same.
REGINA: Well I am
                    the same! For better or for worse I am
                    the same.
DAN: I was always glad to see you,
                    as a kid.
REGINA: That's cause I'm not related
                    to your family—I was normal!
DAN: —Right right!
REGINA: —Ha ha ha!
DAN: And I guess that's why I'm here,
                    I'm trying to sort out—
REGINA: Hold this trash bag
                    open please. It's for Goodwill. Your father
                    was named executor, just to give him
                    something to do. You understand? But then
                    he decided he wanted to manage
                    the whole estate! Like he pictured himself
                    in an office with a secretary
                    and a desk, and the rest of us paying
                    him to do the bookkeeping that the bank
                    was doing anyway! And nobody
                    wanted that. So then they started to go
                    after *me*. I wasted so much money
                    on lawyers, you've no idea. Your parents
                    were scared I'd run away with the money
                    or something. —And I'm really not the type!
                    In fact I watched the money carefully.

But they kept on suing. I've got papers
around here somewhere. They're waiting for me
to kick the bucket cause then they'll get more
money.

DAN: I didn't know that.

REGINA: I've been told
your mother's made, let us say, "inquiries"
about my health lately. But my parents
lived to be a hundred, so your parents
can suck on eggs!

DAN: Ha ha ha.

REGINA: Be a doll
and go get me that suitcase from the bed
in the guest room, will you?

DAN: It seemed crazy
to me, that's all—

REGINA: What's that, dear?

DAN: —The lawsuits!
No matter how often my mother tried
to explain—

REGINA: Your parents became obsessed
about the money. That's all. They became
obsessed!

DAN: And is that cause they didn't have
any money of their own? Cause it seemed
like we were living month to month.

REGINA: That's cause
you were. Would you pack this up for me please?
My arthritis.

DAN: Cause they were both so young
when they got married. When they eloped. Which
is another thing I've always found strange—

REGINA: It was.

DAN: And then they go and buy a house
in Scarsdale—?

REGINA: Well if they had any help
buying that house—I do not want to know
about it.

DAN: Okay.

REGINA: Cause we both did things,
Jim and I. We kept some things to ourselves.
And we had an exceptional marriage
because of it. —But as far as buying
—I can't even remember!

DAN: Cause six kids

is a lot—

REGINA: Even with money six kids
is too many kids! And I remember
you kids doing the housework. Like painting
the walls? tearing out the what—asbestos?
Oh sure. There were lots of suspicious things
going on. And you never had that much
in the kitchen.

DAN: Can I ask you? After
my parents disowned me, or whatever
it was actually, I went to talk to
some therapists.

REGINA: —Oh yeah?

DAN: And they helped me
diagnose my mother as something called
Borderline Personality Disorder.

REGINA: Border what?

DAN: Personality. Disorder.

REGINA: That doesn't sound good.

DAN: It affects people
who grew up in dysfunctional families—

REGINA: Do you have it?

DAN: What? No. I don't think so.
—And the one symptom all these people have,
and they're often women, for what it's worth,
is how they'll switch from like adoring you
to—in the blink of an eye—believing
you're evil incarnate. All cause they're scared
you'll leave them.

REGINA: You know, you might have something
there.

DAN: Cause often these abusive mothers
were abused themselves.

REGINA: Ignored.

DAN: Other kinds
of abuse.

REGINA: Hm.

DAN: So have you ever heard
anything about sexual abuse
in the family—?

REGINA: "Sexual"? —Your mother?
—I don't know, you'd have to ask her!

JAMES: Nancy?

NANCY: I didn't see you, Daddy.

JAMES: Sit with me,   *Night.*

Nancy.

NANCY: But I just got out of the bath,   *In the window,*
I need to get dressed.

JAMES: Come sit beside me.   *the orange*

NANCY: Are you sad?   *oak leaves*

JAMES: It's your mother.   *have turned*

NANCY: Don't be sad.

JAMES: It's your mother. It's your mother. Won't you   *back to green.*
sit with your father, please?

REGINA: —What a question!   *Then just as quickly*
Cause Darcy turned out just fine thank you cause   *it's fall*
she was the baby so everybody   *again.*
just *doted* on her—

DAN: Right.

REGINA: She was with me
since she was thirteen and now look at her
she's sixty! And Gwendolyn turned out sane.
Ilana's always been a head case but
your mother—I just don't think your mother's
had an easy life.

DAN: I don't know.

REGINA: I know
she told her sisters a long time ago
how lucky she's been.

DAN: "Lucky"?

REGINA: But how much
can anybody know about families
you see maybe once a year?

DAN: Which was strange
when you think about it. Cause half the year
you were living right here, which is like what,
twenty minutes away?

REGINA: —Everything bad
that has happened to your family, Danny,
has had to do with the problem of who
your father is.

DAN: Who—?

REGINA: Cause another man
in his situation—I would've worked
three jobs! If I had to. But that's just me
and what do I know, he's your father but
if he'd just stayed what he was, a plumber?
like his father was?—well he could've made
a fortune fixing toilets. But oh no
plumbing wasn't good enough for Harold.

DAN:	He worked as a computer programmer for Pepsi for a while. Before he left to start his own company.
REGINA:	He got fired from Pepsi.
DAN:	He did?
REGINA:	When you are employed by a corporation, you have to shut off your brain. You have to adjust. I used to work in advertising in the sixties cause I like to work. And one day my boss took my hand and said: Don't be smart. Forget everything you know cause now you'll do it my way.
DAN:	Wow.
REGINA:	I said, Fine! What do I care? You want to work, you have to know something about human nature. And your father —Harold, he could never stand being told what to do.
DAN:	Well I think he had a dream of becoming like this white-collar guy. Like Grandpa. Like Jim. He liked to tell us how once upon a time when he was young he woke up one morning and decided that he wouldn't spend the rest of his life up to his elbows in other people's shit.
REGINA:	You know he wanted to get a job with your grandfather's company.
DAN:	—Really?
REGINA:	But they said they weren't hiring family anymore.
DAN:	When was this?
REGINA:	And remember how he'd get all dressed up for work and not *go* anywhere? —If he were my husband I'd be upset!
DAN:	She was.
REGINA:	At least you *try* to do something! You *work!* We can't all be millionaires, right?
DAN:	No.
REGINA:	But she stuck with him through it all. Ever think of that?

DAN: I think
          it's like a lot of victims of abuse:
          on some unconscious level we desire
          the abuse. Seek it out.

REGINA: It stimulates
          your life.

DAN: It becomes an excuse.

REGINA: Mm hm.

DAN: For failure. For not getting a career.

REGINA: —And that's something I never understood.

DAN: Me neither.

REGINA: Cause it's not like she never
          talked about it!

DAN: She went back to college
          a few times. Took classes.

REGINA: And remember
          how one year I bought her that personal
          home computer?

DAN: Her favorite was Memoir
          & Autobiography. Sojourner
          Truth, Maya Angelou. She loved stories
          of subjugation. She always wanted
          to be a writer. Or work in PR,
          or advertising like you. But always
          she'd just flake out. Our father needed her
          at home, she'd say. Not to mention the kids.
          She always acted like she could've been
          Joan Didion or somebody. She'd say
          she had like this genius-level IQ—

REGINA: Oh sure—

DAN: But most of the time she just read
          self-help books. Watched soap operas. *Ryan's Hope*,
          Days of Our Lives. It was just this very
          fifties sort of thing where she'd stay at home
          and my father would be the breadwinner.
          Only problem was—

REGINA: He wasn't winning
          any bread! Ha ha ha!

DAN: Ha ha ha. Yeah.

REGINA: I do feel badly for your mother though,
          I really do. I didn't have any
          daughters. So your mother and her sisters
          were like my daughters and, and, and—as good
          as I've been to your family! Believe me,
          it was me and not your grandfather! —Why

she would do this to me, I will never
understand.

DAN: I'm sorry.

REGINA: Hand me that box
of tissues there. Thank you. —And they were thrilled
with *you*, Danny! Just thrilled!

DAN: I know.

REGINA: What with
college, and all that you got out of it
after, that *fellowship*. Didn't you go
find your roots in Ireland or somewhere?

DAN: Right.

REGINA: —So what happened?

DAN: I wanted to thank you
for paying for college. I fell in love
with my wife there, and started to become
a writer.

REGINA: Well we were glad to help out,
Grandpa and I.

DAN: When I was growing up
my mother always said I was most like
Grandpa. Like Jim. Do you agree?

REGINA: Yes.

DAN: Why?
The way I look or—?

REGINA: The way you look but
something else.

DAN: When my father used to say
I took after Grandpa, he'd say it like
it was something to despise.

REGINA: Your father
was a loser. I'm sorry to have to
tell you. And your grandfather made him feel
inadequate.

DAN: But is it possible
that my father had uh, other reasons
to feel insecure?

REGINA: Oh right, Skippy said
you had this crazy idea—

DAN: You never
heard anything suspicious about my
Uncle Brian?

REGINA: I think it's too late now
to change who your father is.

DAN: Hm.

REGINA: But why
don't you go ask your family, your brothers
and sisters?

DAN: We don't talk to each other
anymore, actually.

REGINA: Well that's too bad
you lost your family, Danny. But maybe
one day—!

DAN: Oh God I hope not.

REGINA: Ha ha ha
okay, time to finish up—

DAN: The thing is
I don't feel much like Grandpa anymore.
I used to feel like him, successful, though
I barely knew him. And I never felt
much like my father. Harold. But lately
I feel like I could be turning into
Harold. Against my will. When I'd rather
be like Grandpa Jim, save for this question
of whether or not he ever abused
my mother. Sorry. I had a few drinks
in the club bar downstairs.

REGINA: Are you drunk now?

DAN: Little bit. Little bit.

REGINA: I think that's sad.
Time to go.

DAN: Do you want my phone number?

REGINA: Does Skip have it?

DAN: Maybe.

REGINA: That's good enough
for me. And take this garbage out with you
please.

5: RACCOONS LIKE BROTHERS

DAN: What am I looking at here?   *Florescence.*

PAUL: Computer
servers. The red lines are the phone lines and   *An office.*
the blue ones are for data.

DAN: It's loud.   *Drone.*

PAUL: What?

DAN: —I said it's so loud!

PAUL: It's the cooling fans!

DAN: Wow!
PAUL: You want to see my new apartment?
DAN: Oh. —Okay.
PAUL: Come on I'll give you a ride

----

            in my new car.   *New car.*
DAN: So you'll be staying here
            for Thanksgiving?   *Overcast.*
PAUL: Well Friday I have to
            take off, so I know I'm going to get like   *Heavy metal*
            real bored real quick. But it's kind of nice to   *music*
            you know, just ah, relax and play *Warcraft*   *low.*
            and stuff? Or just watch like those marathons
            they have on TV all day. *Twilight Zone,*
            The Godfathers, ha ha ha.
DAN: Do you go
            into the city ever?
PAUL: I haven't
            been in the city in years. —Too many
            people! Ha ha ha!
DAN: And do you ever,
            you know, just roll by the old house?
PAUL: What? Why?
DAN: To see what's changed?
PAUL: Uh uh. How about you.
DAN: I was thinking of swinging by today
            but I'm worried the neighbors might worry
            that I'm a child molester or something.
PAUL: —Ha ha ha!
DAN: Do you ever get pressure

----

            to, I don't know, go visit our parents   *Parking lot.*
            in Virginia?
PAUL: Uh uh. How about you.   *Crows cawing.*
DAN: Well you know what happened right?
PAUL: What happened?
DAN: They didn't come to our wedding.
PAUL: Why not?   *Train passing.*
DAN: —She hasn't told you any of this?
PAUL: —No!
DAN: I didn't know if you were back in touch
            with our parents or not or—
PAUL: Well but well
            six years ago I tried to kill myself
            again.

DAN: Okay, I think I knew that.
PAUL: And
for the next couple years I tried all kinds
of medication. In the hospital
the last time I was hallucinating.
DAN: From the what—medication?

PAUL: From withdrawal   *Elevator.*
symptoms. From like this drug that didn't work
for me. Press six please.   *Ding.*
DAN: Cause I've been taking
Zoloft, for anxiety, you know like
obsessions.
PAUL: I tried Zoloft but I'm on
Celexa, Dumyrox, 2 milligrams
of Xanax, which I like.
DAN: Good.
PAUL: Even though
it tends to give me, ah, this dry mouth and
it's made me gain a lot of weight!
DAN: The point
is we all need to figure out which drugs
work best for us.
PAUL: —And it's not anything
embarrassing!
DAN: I know!
PAUL: Everybody
at work knows! My friends! I've had the same job
for like decades—!
DAN: After you.

PAUL: Well but well   *Hallway.*
I was going to say that when I was in
outpatient treatment, the doctors told me   *Dim.*
it's important to like construct yourself
like a support network?   *Buzzing light.*
DAN: Sure.
PAUL: So I called
Mom, and basically just mended fences
with her.
DAN: Wow. Wow.
PAUL: Yeah, and now we'll email
once or twice a year. Like Christmas, birthdays.
But Mom and Dad never invite me down
to visit them, and I'll never invite

myself. Ha ha ha. Okay, this lock sticks
sometimes. And voilà! Welcome to my new

---

apartment! I don't have that much stuff yet   *Apartment.*
but it's real pretty when the leaves are still
on the trees.   *Dark.*

DAN: It's a pretty neighborhood.

PAUL: Sometimes you hear the Metro-North whoosh by   *Train passing.*
but you get used to it. Careful, that paint
is still wet I think. Yeah.

DAN: Did you paint this
yourself or—?

PAUL: No Jocelino helped me
pick out the color in the um, bedroom
—which I really like!

DAN: Who's Jocelino?

PAUL: He's calling right now. Hey, Jocelino!
How's it going? Good good. I just stopped by
to show my brother the apartment. No
it's good! It looks really, really good! Yeah
we're going to go get some lunch. All right, bye
Jocelino!

DAN: Who's Jocelino?

PAUL: He's
a friend. A neighbor. He's a painter.

DAN: Paul,

---

why don't you order first?   *Diner.*

PAUL: May I please have
the French toast, two eggs scrambled with a side   *There's no need*
of bacon? Crispy. Thank you.   *for food,*

DAN: And I'll do
the Amstel Lite. And a veggie burger   *or wait staff either.*
deluxe.

PAUL: Ha ha ha!

DAN: So this is nice! This   *Cloudy*
is more than I think we've ever talked, like   *shop window,*
since we were kids.

PAUL: I don't think we ever   *maybe*
talked then either.   *a drizzle,*

DAN: I think I used to think
you hated me.   *trees losing*

PAUL: —Oh yeah?   *their leaves.*

DAN: Cause I was like
the Golden Boy, or thought I was, and you

weren't.

PAUL: Ha ha ha.

DAN: Like I remember
listening to your footsteps over my head
in your room in the attic, just pacing
back and forth like you were a prisoner,
or creeping down the stairs late at night and
I was sure you were going to kill us all
in our sleep.

PAUL: —Ha ha ha!

DAN: And how you'd sit
at the dining table staring at us
like you hated our guts.

PAUL: I just hated
living there, that's all.

DAN: You know I used to
steal your porno magazines.

PAUL: —I knew that!

DAN: While you were in the shower, or outside
mowing the lawn, I'd sneak into your room
and snoop around. All your dirty laundry,
junk food wrappers, sci-fi and fantasy
paperbacks—

PAUL: Ha ha ha.

DAN: I don't know what
I was looking for really. Aside from
the pornography.

PAUL: —Oh another thing
I hated about our parents is how
they didn't have any boundaries.

DAN: —I know!

PAUL: Ha ha ha.

DAN: So like I emailed you, Paul,
I've been interviewing relatives cause
I've decided to write this play about
our family. Which has to include writing
about family secrets—

PAUL: Well there sure was
a lot of them!

DAN: Like?

PAUL: Like I remember
this one time Mom was real angry at Dad
and she told me, Who do you think pays for
this family? Your father's been unemployed
for months now! —And I'm thinking, Savings. Right?

They must have some savings saved up somewhere,
right? And she tells me: My father gives me
stock in his company, and I sell it
cause your father *forces* me! She's shouting
—*I* am the breadwinner of this family!
And this was like when I was real little
and it was like, so *vicious*. I felt sad,
you know, for Dad.

DAN: She'd use us like a spouse.

PAUL: Oh yeah.

DAN: Against him.

PAUL: Exactly.

DAN: Against
each other too. It was incestuous
in a way.

PAUL: —And remember those raccoons?

DAN: Of course.

PAUL: Cause that night she warned us, Don't go
in the kitchen! Cause your father's sitting
in the breakfast nook cleaning and loading
his rifle!

DAN: Like he's going to execute
every raccoon in town!

PAUL: Cause every night
they'd squeeze through the fence and come scurrying
down this trail they'd worn in the grass and rip
the lids off our garbage cans, and drag out
all our dirty diapers, and the chicken
carcasses and maxi pads—

DAN: Dad's condom
wrappers—

PAUL: And the next morning everything's
strewn out all over the yard. These red piles
of scat. With flies buzzing. You'd pick up rice
with your bare hands and you'd feel the rice move
cause they were like—maggots!

DAN: It was my job
to clean it all up.

PAUL: —It was my job first.

DAN: —Are you sure?

PAUL: And I was thinking maybe
Dad's trying to do me a favor by
taking out a few raccoons.

DAN: —Who knows what
he was ever thinking!

PAUL: But the next day
he's waking me up and saying, Get dressed
and get a baseball bat from the garage
and come round back. —Ha ha ha! And I'm like,
This is not good. Just—not good! But you know
he's like our father so this is serious
business. So I grab the bat and I run
to the backyard and I see this family
of raccoons—just slaughtered. He'd shot them all
during the night, and thought he'd killed them but
in the morning saw some were still breathing
in the grass. Like, paralyzed. He was scared
our neighbors would hear the gunshots during
breakfast. And I don't know if he couldn't
do it himself, or if he wanted to
teach me a lesson, but he said I should
do the bludgeoning. —And I'm like—I can't
do that! You know? —I can't *do* that!

DAN: How old
were you, Paul—?

PAUL: He takes the bat and pulls it
up over his head, like this, like he'll just,
you know—hatchet it down. —But he misses!
—Just hits the dirt!

DAN: Was it still moving or
twitching or was it—?

PAUL: It was like coughing,
choking on blood. And I remember one
was just a baby looking at me when
he crushed its head.

DAN: It's such an obvious
metaphor!

PAUL: —I know! He couldn't even
figure out a raccoon-proof garbage can,
so his solution was to sit up there
like uh, Lee Harvey Oswald—!

DAN: Ha ha ha!

PAUL: When I tell Jocelino this story
he just laughs and laughs and laughs.

DAN: It's funny
cause I remember it like it was me
back there with our father. I can see him
cocking our Louisville slugger above
his bald head. I see my hands on the wood
of the shovel—

PAUL: Right, cause we buried them—
DAN: Under that blooming red azalea bush,
              and how they smelled like wet dogs. And their blood
              looked like jelly. I don't remember you
              there at all. I remember our mother
              telling me this had to be a secret
              we'd die with. Which is the exact same thing
              she said to me the night after you tried
              to kill yourself. We were in the attic
              at the top of the stairs near the window
              you'd jumped from. I'd shown her the note you'd left
              that said, you know, Dear Mom, looks like you'll get
              that playroom you've always wanted. Which meant
              your bedroom could become a playroom for
              the younger kids. And she cried in my arms
              while I was holding her up and she said,
NANCY: This is a secret we must take with us
              to our graves.
DAN: —It's so strange you remember
              a family of them, cause I remember
              two raccoons, like brothers.
PAUL: Ha ha ha!
DAN: Now
              I need to hear *every* story—
PAUL: I've tried
              to block most of it out!
DAN: I'll have a skim
              latte please. Do you want anything else,
              Paul?
PAUL: —And what about Uncle Brian?
DAN: What
              about him?
PAUL: Remember how he left and
              disappeared?
DAN: It's my earliest memory,
              I was three. He was looking down on me
              with those thick glasses like Buddy Holly
              and that long hair and long beard like Jesus
              or Allen Ginsberg—
PAUL: Brian said goodbye
              to *me*.
DAN: No—
PAUL: Cause I would wake up before
              everybody, and I asked him to play
              checkers. And we played. And then he just walked

out the door. —Ha ha ha!

DAN   You sure? Maybe
I'm going crazy, like everybody
else in our family.

PAUL: Well we always thought
there was something wrong with you.

DAN: In what way?

PAUL: You didn't belong. And Dad hated you
the most.

DAN: That reminds me, Paul. Ever since
I broke with our parents, I've been haunted
by this feeling that maybe there's something
that explains everything. And recently
I had this epiphany, or maybe
it was more like a coin dropping: What if
Uncle Brian's my father?

PAUL: Uncle what?

DAN: —It's just an idea.

PAUL: —That would be awesome
if it's true!

DAN: Yeah.

PAUL: —I should get back to work.

DAN: Right, let me get the check.

PAUL: But you're the guest.

DAN: I invited you—

PAUL: But I'm the older
brother!

DAN: Okay. Thank you. And hey, congrats
on the new apartment, by the way. Cause
you seem good. You seem ah, happy. You know
you can always call or um, email me
if you need anything, right?

PAUL: —Well but well
I meant to say he called me once. Brian.

DAN: When?

PAUL: Like in the nineties? I was living
at home still. I don't know where you all were
but Brian was like really, really drunk.
He kept saying he was sorry.

DAN: For what?

PAUL: I don't know. I couldn't understand. Cause
he was slurring his speech and calling me
"Danny." That's what I remember the most:
"Danny."

DAN: Why didn't you ever tell me—?

PAUL: Well I don't think we were really talking
             then.
DAN: Did he say where he was?
PAUL: Florida
             maybe? building movie theaters for Loews
             or something. Ha ha ha. He kept rambling
             on and on and on and eventually
             he started to cry so I just hung up
             on him. Okay, do you need a ride back
             to the train?
DAN: No, I'm going to take a walk
             past the old house today. I'll let you know
             if things look any different.   *Animation:*

6: DEAD ENDS   *line drawing*

DAN: Did you go there, Dan?   *of a seed.*
DAN: You went with me, Dan.
DAN: And what happened?
DAN: We walked down the dead-end
             looking—
DAN: For what?
DAN: Like a child molester
             skulking in the cul-de-sac, skunk cabbage   *The seed growing*
             and wild grape vines,   *like a thread*
DAN: scrub oak and mud-soft weeds   *of water.*
             we used to call The Swamp.
DAN: That brook seething
             with broken bottle glass and rotting leaves,
             rusted car batteries.
DAN: What else was there?
DAN: A haunted house. But smaller. The grass is   *Becoming grass.*
             greener than it was. The dogwood is bare
             and of course taller.   *A tree.*
DAN: This is not the house,
             this has never been the house.
DAN: And then where
             did we go?
DAN: "Old Ridge." Above the thrumming
             of the parkway. Atop the highest hill
             in the county, with a view of the Sound   *The tree*
             on the horizon.
DAN: While landscapers blow   *drops its leaves.*

waves of gold and ruby leaves to the curb.

DAN: Chain-link girds the acreage now. This gate is
all that's left.

DAN: Oxidized green pikes with words
overhead in soldered iron that read
like the entrance to Dante's Inferno:
"Old Ridge."   *Leaves become a*

DAN: Stooping to peer through the shifting
bare branches,   *labyrinth.*

DAN: I'm straining to imagine
the house as it was when my mother was
only a girl,

DAN: and you can't help but feel   *The labyrinth*
you were right. You know you've always been right   *becomes a house*
about her.

DAN: The brick house sprawls. Twin lions   *of dead leaves.*
poised in marble. Sandstone steps. Antique cars
line the driveway.

DAN: The glass of the greenhouse
smears the fire of a November sunset
romantically.

DAN: Somebody else lives here
now.

DAN: Who could possibly live here?

DAN: Should I
ring the bell? Could I just walk inside and
see her twirling in a blue party dress
at the foot of the stairs?

NANCY: You'll never know
how bad it was for me, Danny.

DAN: I know
I've always known the truth.

DAN: A Dalmatian
swivels its ears and leaps barking across
the rolling lawn racing.

DAN: I turn tail and
run for the station laughing.   *This house of*

DAN: So tell me   *dead leaves gets*
what's wrong.   *blown apart.*

DAN: I don't know who to reach out to
next.

DAN: You'll always have me.

DAN: Nobody else
wants to talk to me.

DAN: Why do you want to

talk to them then?

DAN: Cause I've hit this dead end
and I've got to find the truth.

DAN: And to find
the truth you've got to ask people questions

DAN: —and people have to answer them.

DAN: So who
do you want to talk to still? Who is it
that could finally answer this for you?
—Let's go!

DAN: I drive over to Cahuenga   *Los Angeles.*
Boulevard:

ADAM: You want to go off the grid   *Sunlight through*
you can. But it's no piece of cake. E.g.   *Venetian blinds.*
no credit cards, no cell phones. No address
or medical records. *Cash is king.* Wives   *A little*
call me up all the time asking, Adam,   *noir-ish.*
my husband's cheating!—can you surveil him
please? And I'm like, Ma'am, surveillance runs you
two-three hundred an hour. Might I suggest
you go online and look at his statements
cause invariably there's bouquets, bistros
that are inappropriate for business
lunches. Shit like that. It's like—how stupid
can these jagoffs be? It's like I tell them,
Go find yourself a woman you despise
and buy her a McMansion: it's cheaper
than a divorce!

DAN: Ha ha ha!

ADAM: So tell me
who you looking for.

DAN: Brian O'Brien.

ADAM: Sounds like an alias.

DAN: There's good reason
to think he does have a few. Cause he burned
his draft card, I heard. And he used to date
Angela Davis and the Black Panthers
wanted him dead. Was the rumor.

ADAM: You sure
this guy actually exists?

DAN: I hope so.

ADAM: Where was he last seen?

DAN: He made a phone call
from Florida in the nineties.

ADAM: Well hell

that narrows things down a bit. And how old
was he when he disappeared.

DAN: Twenty-five
or so.

ADAM: So he could very well be dead.

DAN: I hadn't thought of that.

ADAM: Where'd he grow up?

DAN: Scarsdale. New York. Where I grew up.

ADAM: —Scarsdale?
—I'm from Great Neck! —Long Island!

DAN: That makes sense
with the accent.

ADAM: —What accent? —Just fucking
with you, Danny!

DAN: You know I can't pay you
anything, or not much.

ADAM: Huh?

DAN: Playwriting's
kind of like being a social worker,
except instead of helping others you
often just help yourself. And even that's
debatable. I could put you in this
play I'm writing.

ADAM: Like what, a cameo
or something? I've always wanted to be
in pictures.

DAN: It's just a play. It might be
a play, one day.

ADAM: So who's this guy to you
anyway?

DAN: My uncle. Though I suspect
there's reason to believe he's my father.
Does that sound nuts?

ADAM: No, it's pretty common
actually. I assume you've asked people
in your family?

DAN: I don't have a family.

ADAM: Like everybody's dead?

DAN: To me they are.
Or I am to them. It's a long story.

ADAM: Another aspect you should consider
is how folks like you just often assume
their uncle or father or whoever's
just sitting around waiting to be found.
When in reality you find this chump

and he's not happy to be found at all,
not at all.

DAN: Yeah.

ADAM: So what I'll need from you
is your uncle's middle name.

DAN: I don't know.
I'm still waiting for a call from Adam.

DAN: So where's that leave us now?

DAN: Awake at night
Googling Brian O'Brien plus different
states, different jobs:

DAN: Brian O'Brien plus
construction worker. Brian O'Brien
plus plumber.

DAN: Have I told you a famous
author once held my hand in the darkness
of his studio in London and said,

FAMOUS BRIT: You have such beautiful hands. I don't mean
to say your hands are womanly. These hands
make things!

DAN: Brian O'Brien ceramist.
Brian O'Brien minor dramatist.
Brian O'Brien homeless suicide.

DAN: Brian O'Brien Brian O'Brien
like a serpent swallowing its own tail.

DAN: I send a letter to everybody
named Brian O'Brien in Florida
and New York cause why not. Then branching out
to the other forty-eight. Then Ireland
cause I've long suspected—

DAN: But what happens
when you find him and he tells you, I'm not
your father. How sad you think so!

DAN: He might
say that. He might say that and be lying,
and if he's a liar or a weirdo
it won't matter, cause at least I'll have found
something worth writing about.

DAN: But what if
he wants money?

DAN Ha ha ha.

DAN: This could bring
new problems. You know that.

DAN: Maybe I'd like
some new problems.

*The branches
again, maybe

like a network

of neurons,

of internet
connections,

ganglia and axons,

nodes and

hubs.*

DAN: Careful what you ask for.

DAN: —Some stories *do* have endings. Some people
get an answer.

GWENDOLYN: Hello? —Hello?   *Sunlight*

DAN: Hello,   *in one*
Aunt Gwendolyn?   *small window,*

GWENDOLYN: Who's this please?

DAN: I told her   *the sun*
what I'd been up to the last twenty years.   *of LA,*

GWENDOLYN: Mmm.

DAN: We discussed the weather of course here   *or sun*
in sunny LA.   *bouncing off*

GWENDOLYN: Mmm.

DAN: You're still living   *snow*
in Connecticut?   *in Connecticut.*

GWENDOLYN: Oh yes. —Not dead yet!

DAN: Ha ha ha.

GWENDOLYN: So what's all this I'm hearing
about you writing a book?

DAN: I explained
that this is a play.

GWENDOLYN: Mmm.

DAN: Yup.

GWENDOLYN: Tell me why
you won't speak to your parents.

DAN: They won't speak
to me, in fact.

GWENDOLYN: Mmm. Mmm.

DAN: They kept saying
I looked like my father's younger brother,
Brian O'Brien. Cause I'd grown a beard
and my hair was longer—

GWENDOLYN: Guess they didn't
like that beard then!

DAN: No. Guess not.

GWENDOLYN: —Ha ha ha!

DAN: But there were other things that made no sense.

GWENDOLYN: Mmm.

DAN: Which of course got me remembering
how they sued you all—

GWENDOLYN: You know what? all that
was so long ago and upsetting that
we just don't talk about it.

DAN: —And thank you
for not hanging up on me—

GWENDOLYN: I'm happy
                 to help you out here, Danny! All I know
                 is that your mother really loved children.
DAN: Huh.
GWENDOLYN: —Well she certainly seemed to!
DAN: She seemed
                 to resent us mostly.
GWENDOLYN: Why would she have
                 six kids then?
DAN: That's my question too.
GWENDOLYN: With you,
                 Danny, she thought you'd become a famous
                 novelist. Or *somebody*.
DAN: She'd tell me
                 how I'd be a writer when I grew up
                 but then she'd beg me not to write about
                 our family. But the way she would beg me
                 kind of sounded like she wanted me to
                 write about us anyway.
GWENDOLYN: Well she had
                 a very peculiar sense of humor,
                 didn't she.
DAN: Did she? Does she?
GWENDOLYN: —I think so,
                 ha ha ha!
DAN: What was it like growing up
                 in that mansion, Old Ridge?
GWENDOLYN: By that you mean
                 how our brother went schizophrenic and
                 our mother became an alcoholic.
DAN: Sure.
GWENDOLYN: Mmm.
DAN: Yes.
GWENDOLYN: Well.
DAN: Was there any other
                 abuse? Like, ah—?
GWENDOLYN: No no no. No no no.
                 No no no no no no no no no no—
DAN: Okay, but—
GWENDOLYN: Hold on a second, Danny.
DAN: You got it.
GWENDOLYN: That was your Uncle Dickie.
                 He's insisting on shoveling the driveway
                 all by himself.
DAN: Oh no.

GWENDOLYN: Remember when
                    he'd take you all out fishing on the Sound?
                    Why don't you write about the happy times
                    instead? How old are you now?

DAN: I'm not sure.

GWENDOLYN: Don't you think it's time you got over this?
                    You're not getting any younger, you know.
                    I had all five of my children before
                    I turned twenty-six!

DAN: Maybe I won't have
                    any kids.

GWENDOLYN: Maybe you can't have kids cause
                    you're still a child yourself. You ever thought
                    of that?

DAN: Yep.

GWENDOLYN: Now you should know your mother
                    got in touch with me a few years ago.

DAN: Oh. Really?

GWENDOLYN: And we send each other cards
                    at Christmas—

DAN: And you just never bring up
                    what happened with the lawsuits?

GWENDOLYN: No we don't
                    ever talk about all that. Mmm.

DAN: Mmm.

GWENDOLYN: Mmm.

DAN: Otherwise it would be hard to chat, right?

GWENDOLYN: And I've got to say, I don't understand
                    any of this! When your mom and I spoke
                    last time, she sounded so happy!

DAN: "Happy"?

GWENDOLYN: She barely mentions you at all, Danny.

DAN: Mmm.

GWENDOLYN: Does she know you're writing a tell-all
                    novel about them?

DAN: It's a fucking play.

GWENDOLYN: What—?

DAN: It's a play. Like in an actual
                    theater with actors and audiences
                    and not a fucking novel. Jesus.

GWENDOLYN: Mmm.

DAN: Sorry.

GWENDOLYN: There's no need for profanity,
                    Danny.

DAN: I apologize.

GWENDOLYN: Did you know
it's your mother's birthday in a few days?
DAN: Oh? Is it?
GWENDOLYN: Why don't you pick up the phone
like you picked up the phone to call me which
I know took some courage, and you tell her,
Mom, hello, I'm writing a "fucking" play
about all our deep dark family secrets
and I'd like to hear your side of things. —See
what she says!
DAN: I've thought about doing that,
but I don't think I'd be able to take
the abuse.
GWENDOLYN: —How do you know it would be
abusive?
DAN: When I say abuse I mean
denial.
GWENDOLYN: Mmm. Mmm. Mmm.
DAN: I should've said *The bright*
she does get in touch with me. I can see
she visits my website a lot, sometimes *window*
several times a day. And she sends emails
once in a while, with photos of foliage *darkens.*
and platitudes about the importance
of family. Or news about accidents
she's had, so call. Or about relatives
I've never met sick with cancer, so please
call. Or about the anniversary
of 9/11 or the Challenger
Disaster. So please call home. With nothing
to say about everything that's happened,
like how they didn't come to our wedding—
GWENDOLYN: But they did come to your wedding, right?
DAN: No.
GWENDOLYN: —They *didn't?*
DAN: No.
GWENDOLYN: —Your mother said they did!
She said you got married in New Hampshire—
DAN: Right.
GWENDOLYN: And they drove up there and how it was
like this tasteful outdoor thing—
DAN: Ha ha ha!
GWENDOLYN: And how your wife's a Hollywood actress
and all the TV shows she's on. —You're *sure*
your mother wasn't there?

DAN: I mean unless
she was hiding up a tree somewhere.

GWENDOLYN: —Why
would she *lie* to me?

DAN: Why don't you ask her?

GWENDOLYN: —Well I don't know if I can help you with
anything else, Danny—

DAN: It's been helpful
just to hear you say "I don't know."

GWENDOLYN: —Happy
writing!

DAN: Bye.

DAN: Well you can't really blame her,
can you? She doesn't know you.

DAN: She doesn't
trust me.

DAN: Should she? She has no idea what
you're writing. It's almost unconscionable
for you to raise the specter of incest
in your mother's family, as compelling
as you might find that—

DAN: It's pretty common
actually.

DAN: You know you're just going to hurt
everybody who's been kind enough to
speak with you.

DAN: But nobody's going to care
about these people if I don't reveal
um, their faults—

DAN: Are you revealing enough
of your own faults though?

DAN: Like which faults, Dan?

DAN: What
about your marriage?

DAN: —I'm not going to write
about—

JESS: All I need is for my husband   *Night*
not to say it feels awful to hug me!   *in the window.*

DAN: I did not say that!

JESS: —I can picture it,   *Moon*
Dan!   *above*

DAN: The meaning of that—we've discussed this   *palm trees.*
a thousand times—

JESS: I am behaving like
a normal person!

DAN: But you know you're *not*
a normal person, right?

JESS: What?

DAN: Cause you have
too much anxiety.

JESS: —*I* do?

DAN: —Yes you
know this!

JESS: I was hoping to be helpful
tonight, Dan. Honestly.

DAN: —But the point is
that's too much *pressure* for you!

JESS: I don't feel
stressed out about your family.

DAN: What's different
about tonight then? What's different is that
I spoke to somebody I haven't seen
in like two decades, somebody who sounds
alarmingly like my mother. That cold
voice. That same spooky denial. —And that
has got to be unsettling!

JESS: —To me?

DAN: —To
anybody! —And you're freaked! —And that's why
I said I wanted to go out alone
tonight. Cause I seem to have two choices:
one is I struggle to keep my distance
and be your therapist—

JESS: I don't want that.

DAN: Which can come across as condescending.

JESS: Cause it is.

DAN: Or instead I ah, engage
and start screaming!

JESS: —I didn't want you to
scream at me like that.

DAN: But you started it.

JESS: I went into my room—

DAN: It's my room too!

JESS: —To get *away* from you!

DAN: You slammed the door
to say fuck you to me!

JESS: No I never
said fuck you!

DAN: —You did! You did! You didn't
say it literally but you said—

JESS: And you
came into the room screaming—
DAN: I did not
scream! I am very cognizant of not
raising my voice at you!
JESS: You spoke—
DAN: Listen
to me.
JESS: In this crazy voice—
DAN: Shut up.
JESS: You
were screaming, Shut the fuck up! You're the one
I found standing in the kitchen stabbing
the cutting board with our most expensive
wedding knife!
DAN: And I'm sorry about that.
JESS: Well I'm telling you now, and we can talk
about this tomorrow but I don't feel
I'm the one with the problem here. I feel
I *am* managing my emotions,
thank you very much—
DAN: Do you truly think
if you hadn't lost your temper at me
first—that *I* would've gotten mad?
JESS: You know
what I truly think, Dan? I think that if
you feel like somebody is telling you
that something's your fault, that any of this
could possibly be your fault? It hurts you
deeply—
DAN: It doesn't—
JESS: And I don't know if
it's your parents' fault cause they abused you
verbally, I don't know if it's just cause
you have unresolved issues with women
cause your mother collapsed in your arms when
she came home from the hospital after
your brother tried to kill himself and said,
Nobody must know! And I don't know if
you're digging up all this shit and talking
to toxic relatives cause you just can't
accept what I know is hard to accept,
which is that your father is your father
and he's an unredeemable person
and your mother's just as bad and they're not

ever going to love you! And your uncle
is just your uncle. Newsflash. Your uncle
is nobody. —And when I tell you that
I'm angry at you, you act like I'm part
of the same fucking family!

DAN: —Stop crying.

JESS: —I can't!

DAN: I'm sorry.

JESS: —I have a marriage
that isn't working!

DAN: We know the reason
for that, don't we?

JESS: Do we?

DAN: Don't we?

JESS: Know what,
babe? Let's put an end to this. Why don't you
go see a movie. Are you crying? Why
are you crying?

DAN: I'm not.

JESS: I'm going to go
to bed.

DAN: Love you.

JESS: Love you.

DAN: That night I call   *Now just one*
a psychic in London.   *palm tree*

BRENDA: I must confess
I'm contending with a bowel complaint   *in the moonlit*
ugh, this morning.   *window.*

DAN: Okay.

BRENDA: But let's see where
this leads us, shall we? Is Father dead please?

DAN: My father?

BRENDA: Yes or no please.

DAN: I'm not sure.

BRENDA: It's just that I've got this gentleman here
from Father's line—

DAN: "Colwell."

BRENDA: Sorry?

DAN: Colwell's
my grandmother's maiden name. —I forgot
till just now.

BRENDA: And have there been any storms
where you are please?

DAN: The rest of the country's
had some snow, I think—

BRENDA: Cause what I'm seeing
is like a hurricane. With a broken   *That palm tree*
palm tree. —I don't know what to make of this,   *bobbing gently*
I honestly don't! —Unh. —Ah-h.
DAN: Brenda?   *in the moonlit*
Are you still there?   *window.*
BRENDA: Do you know what?
DAN: No what.
BRENDA: This isn't working.
DAN: She says my mother's
somehow blocking the reading.
BRENDA: —Ungh.
DAN: Secrets
my mother's been keeping.
BRENDA: Things should just flow
but instead I keep running into these
dead ends.
DAN: —But should I believe some of what
you *did* say, Brenda?
BRENDA: —Oh! yes! please! Believe
everything I've said, ha ha ha!
DAN: I'm right
in believing that I've never known who
my father is.
BRENDA: Yes.
DAN: My true father.
BRENDA: No.
DAN: And he lives in Florida. —Is that fair
to say?
BRENDA: I'm seeing a broken palm tree,
that's all I can give you.
DAN: That's good.
BRENDA: —"Mickey."   *That palm tree*
DAN: Who?   *bobbing*
BRENDA: Your father's father, this gentleman   *in the window*
waiting here so patiently, just whispered
"Mickey" quite distinctly in my ear.   *as dawn is*
DAN: Huh.   *slowly*
BRENDA: Does the name Mickey mean something?
DAN   Maybe.   *breaking.*
BRENDA: Urnh. —Got to go! Cheerio!
DAN: Cheerio!
DAN: It's like
even the spirit world won't talk to you
anymore.

DAN: It's only a dream, a wish
DAN: about Brian. Your secrets follow you
           underground.
DAN: I thought she had a few things
           of value to share.
DAN: Like what?
DAN: Dear Adam:
           you've probably forgotten about me but
           I've just remembered some information
           you might need: my grandmother's maiden name
           was Colwell, which also happens to be
           Brian's middle name.
ADAM: Dan, I was wondering
           what happened to you. Give me half an hour
           to dig some shit up. Hey, it was easy   *That seedling*
           tracking him down. You sure you've been looking   *again*
           hard for this guy? He lives in Hollywood,
           Florida.   *growing*
DAN: Like I live in the other
           Hollywood, or nearby.   *into tendrils*
ADAM: He's a Cancer,   *growing*
           if you're curious. His high school yearbook's   *into*
           online, a senior portrait
DAN: with long hair,   *long hair and*
           glasses, a wisp of mustache   *mustaches,*
ADAM: and a quote
           from the Swiss philosopher-aphorist
           Henri Amiel: "Moral indifference is
           the malady of the cultivated
           class."
DAN: That definitely sounds like him.
ADAM: I'll send
           the bill for my cameo. I can't wait
           to see this picture!
DAN: I see Brian's house   *then mustache-tendrils*
           on my computer screen. Four blocks away
           from the Atlantic, like I live twenty
           from the Pacific. There's a peeling fence   *growing into*
           like a balustrade festooned with kudzu,   *vines,*
           twin lions or maybe gargoyles crouching
           on plinths on either side of a carless
           driveway. Desultory lawn chairs. Trash cans
           toppled in front of the closed garage. Blinds
           drawn. An empty garden trellis looming   *and then something*
           over a concrete stoop. Front door's obscured   *like a storm*

by a battered palm tree.   *-tossed palm.*

DAN: So you write him—

DAN: Dear Mr. O'Brien: I'm researching
a play on the O'Briens of Scarsdale—

DAN: A couple days pass and Hollywood,
Florida visits your website. Clicks through
all your accomplishments, your vanities
and insecurities.

DAN: Then the next night
the same person in Hollywood returns
to my website,

DAN: only to the page with
your picture, this time.

DAN: Several times that night,
then several more times the next.

DAN: And always
only to look at your picture. He goes
every night after that.

DAN: This same person
in Hollywood goes over and over
for weeks now,

DAN: as if studying your face
for something.

DAN: Some proof. Evidence.

DAN: As if
he's not sure what to do next.

DAN: Every night
he returns,

DAN: and every night you brighten
like you're falling in love.

DAN: —Then just like that   *The palm is*
he's gone.   *wiped away.*

DAN: —See? He doesn't care about you.

DAN: Why should he?

DAN: Remember? You're nobody
to him.

DAN: I'm nobody. Just like he is.

DAN: He's not your father. It's just some stalker.

DAN: I've got a stalker?

DAN: A computer glitch
somewhere.

DAN: A dream. Delusion. Our secrets
taken to the grave.

DAN: A computer voice
answers when you call.

DAN: Hello this is um
                  your nephew. I sent you a letter and
                  I'm hoping you might be willing to ah
                  talk.

DAN: Nobody calls back. Nobody's called
                  for months now.

DAN: Why won't he call—?

DAN: There's a way
                  to make this all make sense.

DAN: How?

DAN: Why don't you
                  listen to what everybody's trying
                  to tell you?   *Light*

DAN: My older sister Joyce pens   *grows brighter.*
                  an email:

JOYCE: Ms. Blickers:

DAN: That's my agent.

JOYCE: I am growing increasingly concerned
                  with what my brother is planning to write
                  about our family. From what I have heard
                  from others my brother has interviewed:
                  He is not being truthful.

DAN: That sentence
                  makes no sense to me:

JOYCE: He is not being
                  truthful.

DAN: Joyce has gone years without speaking
                  to our parents. She'd feud with my mother
                  all the time. They kicked her out of the house
                  when she was just out of school, for being
                  depressed. They didn't go to her wedding
                  either. Months before writing my agent
                  she sent me a card she'd designed herself,
                  a letterpress tree denuded of leaves
                  that she's selling on Etsy:

JOYCE: And I hope
                  you'll think twice about the damage, Danny,
                  this play will wreak on our aged parents,
                  but also on your nieces and nephews.
                  And your children, should you ever have some.
                  Writers have a responsibility
                  to tell the truth, yes, but they also have
                  a responsibility not to hurt
                  those they love. Or used to love. Sincerely,

DAN: "He is not being truthful."

JOYCE: your sister
                  Joyce.
DAN: When she was young Joyce aspired to be
                  a painter. Or a writer.
DAN: It's shameful
                  to gripe, Dan. —Move on. Grow up.
DAN: My mother
                  visits my website five, six, seven times
                  a day.
DAN: It's easy.
DAN: A feeding frenzy—
DAN: Don't write anymore.
DAN: It's like they're planning
                  something. —Maybe they're planning to tell me
                  the truth?
DAN: Just stop. Stop writing.
DAN: —Just tell me
                  the truth! —I'm ready!
DAN: Don't say anything
                  when anybody asks you what happened
                  to your family. Or tell them a story—
DAN: Aren't I though?
DAN: —if you can't tell the truth.
                  Close your eyes, go back to sleep.
DAN: My mother
                  sends a sympathy card. This charcoal dove
                  above the printed message:
NANCY: In memories
                  we embrace those we have lost. For the heart
                  will never forget.
DAN: Not a handwritten
                  word of her own. Save for the farewell,
NANCY: Love,
                  Mom & Dad.
DAN: Love,
DAN: love,
DAN: love,
DAN: love.
DAN: Dear Brian:
                  I'm writing you another letter cause
                  I wasn't being entirely truthful
                  with you before. My earliest memory
                  is you. Looking down on me, giving me
                  a children's Bible the morning you left
                  our house in Scarsdale. But who knows maybe

I imagined all this? imagined you
cause the family myth of you, somebody
rebellious and artistically inclined
leaving his family behind—all of this
was something I could identify with
if not aspire to.

BRIAN: THANKS FOR THE INVITE
TO THE DANCE DANNO.

DAN: He emails. All caps
as if shouting across the chasm of
thirty years. Or like a telegram from
a lunatic asylum.

BRIAN: IM HAPPY
TO SEE YOU MADE IT PAST THE AGE OF THREE
AND DONE SO SPLENDIDLY. HA HA HA. BUMMED
TO HEAR ALL THIS STURM-N-DRANG AND BULLSHIT
WITH YOUR FOLKS BUT ITS A RECURRING THEME
IN THIS FAMILY. ENOUGH SAID. CHUG-AND-GO
MY AWFULLY WEDDED WIFE KNEW WHO YOU WERE
FROM THAT PICTURE ON YOUR WEBSITE YOUR HANDS
ARE DEFINITELY OBRIEN HANDS THESE HANDS
UNCLOG DRAINS HAMMER NAILS GUT FISH THANK GOD
YOUR MOMMA DIDNT HAVE THAT BALDNESS GENE
CAUSE IT WOULDNT FIT A HAUNTED IRISH
PLAYWRIGHT! HA HA HA. I HAD A HANDLE
ON THE OBRIEN CLAN LONG TIME PASSING
BLUNTLY SPEAKING MY BIG BROTHER HAROLD
IS A DIRT BAG FOR LETTING THIS HAPPEN
TO YOU AND YOUR FAMILY WITH CERTAINTY
HE LET THIS HAPPEN!!! NO MYTH I AM WHO
YOU ALWAYS PERCEIVED ME TO BE! I MARCH
TO THE BEAT OF MY OWN DRUM HA HA HA
TIME IS ON MY SIDE IVE GOT SCADS OF IT
SO WHY DONT WE RATTLE A FEW BONES WHEN
YOU COME FOR A VISIT? WITH THE IRISH
ITS ALWAYS A GOOD IDEA TO BEGIN
WITH ENVY.

7: SLIT THE FENCES

DAN: First let me just say how crazy this feels   *Sunset,*
               to be finally sitting here with you,
               Brian. What with that palm tree out front—   *Florida,*

BRIAN: Yeah
        I've been meaning to get to that.   *a battered palm tree*
DAN: Your face
        I remember. Your face is the same.   *in a wide window*
BRIAN: Dan,
        seriously? I'm sixty! And what are you,   *in the breeze*
        thirty-seven?
DAN: Exactly.
BRIAN: You look like
        you need a drink. But all I got is skunked
        Budweiser.
DAN: That'll do.
BRIAN: Mind if I smoke?
DAN: And thanks for letting me drop by like this
        on such short notice—
BRIAN: Hey, Danno! —Listen!
        I've been hiding in plain sight all my life!
        —Ha ha ha! Cause this might sound strange to you,
        be careful it's all shook up, *l'chaim*,
        but for a good percentage of my life
        I was vice-president of the largest
        interior construction company
        in the United States.
DAN: Really?
BRIAN: Oh yeah!
        We did Marriotts, United Artists
        theaters. I've spent my entire adult life
        bouncing around the country doing jobs
        in Chicago, California, Texas.
        Our HQ was downtown on Hudson Street
        so I'd be in New York like once a month
        for years. But I'll tell you what: I never
        set foot in Scarsdale since the day I said
        goodbye to you. —And I did say goodbye
        to you, I'm sure of that. I don't know why
        you remember me giving you that what,
        that *Bible*—?
DAN: I don't know why either.
BRIAN: Cause
        I'm not into religion. Though Jesus
        was a right-on dude. If he actually
        existed I mean, ha ha ha!
DAN: So why
        did you just disappear? Why didn't you
        ever visit again?

BRIAN: I remember
the last time I saw your parents, I said
to myself: It's high time I hit the road.
It's like in the Yiddish: Keep your tsuris
in your own backyard. Cause it was real clear
these two had enough tsuris of their own.
Get me?

DAN: All we ever heard about you
were like these legends—

BRIAN: Guilty as charged, man!
Guilty as charged!

DAN: So they're all true?

BRIAN: Oh sure!
Oh sure! We slit the fences in Newport—

DAN: You slit the?—sorry?

BRIAN: —Slit the fences, man!

DAN: —Oh! —Nice!

BRIAN: And it's like this really weird thing
cause it's called the Newport Jazz Festival—

DAN: Right—

BRIAN: But there wasn't ever any jazz!
You had your Janis Joplin, Jethro Tull—

DAN: I love *Aqualung*—

BRIAN: But we didn't have
any tickets. Get me? What we did have
was a pair of Bill Schlitz's post-cutters
—Slit The Fences, man! —Ha ha ha!

DAN: Who's Bill—?

BRIAN: Oh shit poor son-bitch is dead.

DAN: I'm sorry.

BRIAN: Schlitz was old SDS muscle. Get me?

DAN: Um—

BRIAN: And Abbie Hoffman was just some kid
who didn't get enough bar mitzvah cash
ha ha ha! But Schlitz now there was a man
who liked pills and girls. A potentially
lethal combo, brother! Want another
beer there, boyo?

DAN: Please.

BRIAN: —Heads up!

DAN: Did you date
Angela Davis? That was another
rumor.

BRIAN: Shit Sherlock, where'd you hear that one?

DAN: From my mother.

BRIAN: How is she by the way?
              Nancy. Still crazy?
DAN: As far as I know.
BRIAN: Well in this instance she was being straight
              with you, Danny. I rolled with Bobby Seale.
              Angie. Eldridge Cleaver. —This ain't no joke!
              Bobby Seale was one stone-cold mofo, see?
              Not that the FBI's any better:
              they go after you, man, you're toast. Steer clear
              of the legal system in this country,
              that's my advice to you, young man. That and
              Slit The Fences. —Don't Look Back!
DAN: So I guess
              that's why I'm here—
BRIAN: You've got to understand
              something about your family: everything
              goes back to my childhood.
DAN: —*Your* childhood?
BRIAN: Cause
              essentially I should've never been
              born. —Ha ha ha!
DAN: You okay?
BRIAN: Ha ha yeah
              it's just a smoker's cough cause as this late
              -in-life baby, AKA The Mistake,
              AKA The Gift From God, nobody
              was going to pay any attention to
              The Little Turd. But I was sure as shit
              going to pay attention to *them*. Get me?
DAN: So what you're saying—
BRIAN: Cause the greatest gift
              my family ever gave me was the gift
              of listening.
DAN: Right—
BRIAN: I thank them every day.
DAN: But—
BRIAN: They taught me how to *listen!* To see
              what's *really* going on, all around me.
              And for me, the answer to your question
              —What happened to my family?—is simple:
              It's your father. It's your father.
DAN: I know.
BRIAN: —It wasn't our parents' fault.
DAN: It wasn't—?
BRIAN: It wasn't *our* parents' fault!

DAN: But wasn't
                  your mother an alcoholic?
BRIAN: The truth,
                  Dan? Sure she was. Sure she was. Was it bad
                  when Harold and Johnny were growing up?
                  Probably not. Was it something to deal with
                  when I was a kid? You bet. Did she drink
                  after my father had a heart attack
                  in his sleep, which was a real ballbuster
                  by the way? —You bet your white ass she did!
                  —Why'd she stop? —Hey Gertie, you get sober
                  for a reason? you go to AA? Nope.
                  —She couldn't even be a normal drunk!
                  —Like go to rehab a few hundred times!
                  Screw up like the rest of us! But oh no,
                  she just stopped going to the liquor store
                  all the sudden. She was like me. A real
                  odd duck.
DAN: So if it's not your parents' fault,
                  why do you think my father—?
BRIAN: It's Stradone
                  in County Cavan by the way. That's where
                  your grandmother's family's from. The Colwells
                  of Cavan. And you must never forget
                  these people were shanty Irish. You know
                  what I mean by shanty, right? Cause Stradone's
                  just a fork in the road, the gene pool's like
                  a wading pool. They could've used a few more
                  raping Norsemen in that town ha ha ha
                  ha ha ha ha ha ha ha ha ha pass
                  me my water will you?
DAN: Here.
BRIAN: Thank you much
                  better. But see it's the O'Brien branch
                  of the family you got to watch out for,
                  with all that racist King's Point Brooklyn Bronx
                  rum runners priests nuns gangsters anything
                  to make a buck—"You git yer smokes, boyo?
                  you git yer smokes?"
DAN: —Ha ha ha!
BRIAN: Very mean
                  son-bitches too. Resentful. Paranoid
                  like Harold, actually.
DAN: So his problem
                  is that he's Irish—?

BRIAN: If you asked Harold,
              Where's the Abbey Theatre? He'd answer, Huh?
              —Now I happen to think that's a problem!
              —Harold: Seamus Heaney. —Huh?
DAN: Ha ha ha.
BRIAN: Oh yeah. Oh yeah. And who can blame him? Cause
              the nuns were perverse. And Brother Who's-it,
              now there was a sadist. Then Harold's off
              to Scarsdale High School where he finds himself
              in algebra with Liza Minnelli
              and the progeny of Leonard Bernstein
              and Mr. IBM, What's it, Watson,
              and your mother's father too. Real captains
              of industry, man! —But you want to know
              the truth? Of course you do. If you could pry
              it out of Harold with like a crowbar
              and a nuclear bomb—?
DAN: Ha ha ha.
BRIAN: Your dad
              wanted to be a writer.
DAN: You're kidding.
BRIAN: —Oh yeah! —*Oh* yeah!
DAN: —That's crazy.
BRIAN: —And *Beowulf?*
              He loved *Beowulf!* Cause it's true he could be
              extremely sensitive. You had to be
              extremely careful around Harold cause
              you could offend him quite easily cause
              his perceptual screens were all screwed up.
DAN: Yes.
BRIAN: But we Irish are not the most careful
              of people.
DAN: No.
BRIAN: We're the kings of flying
              non sequiturs, we say stuff off the cuff
              we don't really mean. We don't mean to hurt,
              by and large. But when we *do* mean to hurt
              we blow up the Cock and Bull in London.
DAN: Right.
BRIAN: But when all's said and done, I'll admit
              Harold was always exceedingly kind
              to me.
DAN: —What?
BRIAN: Oh yeah! I happen to think
              your dad's a great guy!

DAN: —I don't understand.
BRIAN: Oddly enough, considering the fucking
                lunatic he's become!
DAN: —But what happened?
                Something *must* have happened. Like somebody
                betrayed my father. Some long-ago hurt
                that lingered and festered—
BRIAN: He fell in love.
DAN: Huh.
BRIAN: He fell in love. He fell in love. Now
                here's a story you won't find surprising:
                Harold didn't have a date to the prom.
                So our big brother Johnny took pity
                on him and set him up as a blind date
                with his friend Ilana's sister Nancy.
                And it's like Bibbidi-Bobbidi-Boo,
                everybody's running around searching
                for a tuxedo and a corsage—well
                the deal got sealed that night. Cause it was love
                at first sight.
DAN: It's hard to imagine them
                that way.
BRIAN: Seriously, Danny? Seriously?
                —Love's not an adequate word—*obsession*
                is more like it. Like rabid rabbits—
DAN: Gross.
BRIAN: And Momma Gertrude, smart bag that she was,
                she knew exactly what was happening.
                Harold, keep it in your Jockeys! Or words
                to that effect. Cause this thing was too quick,
                everybody felt that way. But your mom
                was one mean breeding machine.
DAN: Is that why
                they eloped? cause my mother got pregnant
                by accident—?
BRIAN: All I can tell you,
                Danny, is that your father's always been
                secretive. And so's your mother. —*So is*
                your mother.
DAN: Did my mother's father buy
                the house we grew up in?
BRIAN: —No! —You genius!
DAN: Right.
BRIAN: —You figured that out all by yourself?
                Ha ha ha!

DAN: I know.
BRIAN: I'm being flippant
            with you here, Danny. I understand. Cause
            sometimes the hardest thing to figure out
            is what's staring you right in the face.
DAN: Yeah.
BRIAN: Things having to do with *who you are*.
DAN: Yeah.
BRIAN: You're a real perceptive guy. I can tell.
DAN: So are you.
BRIAN: We're similar: both of us
            have empathy. It's why I went into
            contracting and not psychiatry. Cause
            my dream was to shrink people but feelings
            can be a detriment in that field.
DAN: Sure.
BRIAN: And your parents wouldn't know empathy
            if it hit them in the face like a brick.
DAN: That's true.
BRIAN: The love gene's unfortunately
            been twisted up a bit too tightly in
            the what's-in-it-for-me? gene.
DAN: Ha ha ha.
BRIAN: Your parents are basically psychopaths,
            by the way. —Ha ha ha! —Oh, by the way!
            "By the way"—your parents are basically
            psychopaths! —And you must never forget
            what a true psychopath is: they rarely
            kill with bullets. They rarely slit your throat.
            They deprive. They shame. They tear your heart out
            of your chest, look at it and stick it back
            in the wrong way. They do everything but
            pull the trigger. You know why? They're too scared
            to lose you.
DAN: Well they've lost me now.
BRIAN: Have they?
DAN: Growing up I always felt like Harold
            hated me, but I never understood
            why. I used to think maybe it was cause
            I liked joking around, I like people
            sometimes. And he found that strange.
BRIAN: He didn't
            find it strange, Danny—he was envious
            of you! That's what he wanted to do! Who
            he wanted to be!

DAN: The last time we spoke
          he *did* seem jealous—
BRIAN: Cause you've done something
          with your life! —I was telling Chug-and-Go
          last night—If this kid came from *my* pecker?
DAN: He told me I looked like you.
BRIAN: Oh yeah right.
DAN: The hair, the beard—
BRIAN: He never understood
          any of that.
DAN: He kept shouting at me
          —There are things you do not know! —There are things
          you don't know!
BRIAN: Well he kind of had a point
          there, don't you think?
DAN: You tell me.
BRIAN: —Ha ha ha!
DAN: You have any kids, Brian?
BRIAN: Never did.
          —But I got about a dozen bastards
          spread out all over the world! Ha ha ha!
          —That's the way to do it, man!
DAN: Ha ha ha.
BRIAN: You want the truth? Of course you do. That's why
          you're here. No, I never had any kids
          but over the years we've adopted some
          here and there. Unofficially. Lost boys
          and girls a lot like you ha ha ha but
          no, much to my chagrin, the whole kid thing
          never happened. I'm an alcoholic.
DAN: Right.
BRIAN: But I'm like this weird kind of drinker?
          Like say you've got a test or a party
          but you can't do either without taking
          a few belts? What am I? Alcoholic.
          It's not quantity, it's the compulsion
          behind it. —Get me?
DAN: Sure.
BRIAN: You sure you're sure?
          You should be careful. Cause it's in your blood,
          the tendency.
DAN: I know.
BRIAN: And Chug-and-Go
          saved my life. She likes to tell me, Mickey,
          you never met a bottle of Bushmill's

you couldn't drain dry.

DAN: —She calls you Mickey?

BRIAN: Oh yeah. Mick, Mickey. My father called me
Mickey all the time. Nobody calls me
Brian. You look surprised.

DAN: I am surprised,
Mickey.

BRIAN: —You wrote me you had a question
for me? Something that was more important
than the other questions? About me?

DAN: Right.

BRIAN: Hit me.

DAN: I think you answered everything.

BRIAN: Did I?

DAN: Yeah, no—everything makes sense now.

BRIAN: You sure?

DAN: Yes.

BRIAN: Well hey—sounds like you're pulling
something off with your life. Had a few knocks
and you're trying to make sense of it all
and that's cool, brother. Cool. That's what you got
to do, man. I'm not good at kissing ass
and believe it or not some people don't
care for me much—they're like, God damn it, who?
Mickey? —That loud-mouthed pig-fuck?

DAN: Ha ha ha.

BRIAN: But listen—boom. You can bat for my team
any day. You need a glass of water?

DAN: Please.

BRIAN: The thing you must always keep in mind
is that it's always about what they did
to themselves. When you got a mess of kids.
Get me? Who are completely innocent.
Get me? That you got a chance to *give* to?
And then you go and give it your best shot
to screw them over? —Well I don't know what
to call that.

DAN: I don't know either.

BRIAN: Drink this.
—And they'll never say sorry. —They'll never
say they're sorry.

DAN: I know.

BRIAN: And I'm sorry
about that, Danny. I really am. But
the way I see it is you can see life

as some kind of sorrowful negative
like, Oh poor me! and, Why did they have to
do this to me? Or you go, You know what?
that wasn't easy but I got something
out of it. Cause I think about the good
and the bad I've encountered in *my* life?
—I did this to me. —It's all mine, baby!
I own this pain!

DAN: Right.

BRIAN: You went to college,
you got to grow up in God damned Scarsdale,
New York. You get to spend your life scribbling
poems and plays. And you're still here, still breathing,
which may sound obvious but it's not really
when you're as old as me, the same age when
my father died. And also my pecker
doesn't work well. And I got glaucoma
in this eye. But as my second mother
Esther Weiss used to say: It's a mitzvah
they had you at all.

DAN: Yes.

BRIAN: —But they never
should've gotten married.

DAN: No.

BRIAN: They never
should've had children.

DAN: No.

BRIAN: Lucky for us
they did.

DAN: Ha ha ha.

BRIAN: So you'll be staying
for dinner, right?

DAN: I can't.

BRIAN: But Mama Bear's
on her way home—!

DAN: I know but my flight leaves
in a few hours—

BRIAN: Why don't you just crash here
on the couch—or there's a what-you-call-it
crouton somewhere—

DAN: It's been great meeting you
as an adult.

BRIAN: Oh. Okay. —That's cool, man.

DAN: —I can't thank you enough. Really.

BRIAN: —You're free,

Danny! Get out of here!

DAN: Right!

BRIAN: Everything
you've heard about me is true! All the myths
are true!—mostly! Ha ha ha!

DAN: —Ha ha ha!

BRIAN: What's that old line? It never gained on me,
baby. —Cause hey listen: I got lucky.
You want the truth, Danny? Of course you do.
I got lucky the moment I walked out
the door. Get me?

DAN: Yeah.

BRIAN: Have a safe flight back
to that other Hollywood.

DAN: I'm going
to Ireland, actually.

BRIAN: —Huh?

DAN: My brother
Paul—we're meeting up tomorrow morning
in Dublin, renting a car and driving
all over the country, getting in touch
with our roots. Ha ha ha.

BRIAN: Well raise a glass
to your Uncle Mickey in the homeland,
baby.

8: GO AWAY WITH YOU

DAN: Landing before sunrise with my brother
—he's lost,   *Dawn, Ireland,*

DAN: so you pretend you're not.

DAN: And drive
into the west,   *mist that slowly*

DAN: where you'd been an artist
of promise, fifteen years ago traveling
through a dream then too.

DAN: This morning riding   *burns away into*
rented bikes on Inis Mór,

DAN: breathing in
the circus smell of cow dung in the midst
of waves of cycling German teen-tourists
who scream, Up your ass!

DAN: And I'm watching as

my depressive brother edges toward
the cliff,

DAN: as he peers over a pounding
surf.   *a bright light.*

DAN: I'm wondering,
DAN: Will he jump?
DAN: Then laughing
we take selfies in a meadow beside
a doll's house, incongruous and rotting
in the sea-salt mist.

DAN: —You didn't ask him.
DAN: —Why couldn't I ask my Uncle Brian
the answer to my question?

DAN: In Galway
we drink into the night with an old friend
who tells you of his divorce, the aging
of his parents.

DAN: He says,
FRIEND: I remember
you as you were then, Dan. You had this air
of a young man with so many secrets
inside himself. And I see I was right
about that.

DAN: Drunkenly I cry, We're all
being used by the spirit of the truth
that's destroying us!

FRIEND: —Go away with you!
DAN: he laughs down an alleyway.
FRIEND: Go away
with the two of yous! you wandering brothers,
you twin apostates!

DAN: —Go away with all
secrets and shame and lies and guilt!

FRIEND: —Farewell!
DAN: —Farewell!
FRIEND: Farewell! Farewell! —Farewell!
DAN: Hung over
the next morning while breakfasting on beans
and eggs toast rashers white sausage and blood
sausage too, my brother tells me, Last night
I had a dream I was back in the house
we grew up in. And everybody saw
your name on the TV screen and I begged
our mother, Why can't you apologize
to him? Sundry sightseeing excursions

ensue. More stout and sausage, turf and coal
fire and this unseasonable sun. I don't
deserve this, my brother says. Driving through
canary gorse and sparkling bog. This place
speaks to me. Speaks to me. I say, We're free
of who we were born to be. And he feels
sick. Feels ill. He feels certain he will die
too soon. So I lie and say happiness
means we're all dying too soon. Take a nap
and then a shower. And this boat ride out
to Skellig Michael, my brother and I
on a blue exhaust cloud with the ancient
skipper Joe Roddy and more Dutch tourists
beneath the observant yolk-faced gannets,
past Little Skellig, that stark cathedral
of gulls gossiping on guano-stained cliffs,
and farther still, to the triangle skull
of Skellig Michael. Where Sixth Century   *Bright, bright*
monks carved out these hundreds of time-worn steps   *light.*
to an islandtop of stone huts like tombs
or hives or ovens in the burning light,
each stride we take another burning stripe
of penance. I'm sorry. He asks me, Why
can't you be the one to apologize
even if you don't mean it? We lie down
to rest on this slanted strand of lichen
-spotted limestone, with the seabirds circling
above our faces and the proud senseless
sea.

END OF PLAY

NEW LIFE

New Life was commissioned and developed by Center Theatre Group in Los Angeles, and supported by a Guggenheim Fellowship in Drama & Performance Art.

New Life has received development with the New Harmony Project, the LA Writers' Workshop Festival at Center Theatre Group, and PlayLabs at The Playwrights' Center.

New Life was excerpted with the title "Long Days" in the *Sewanee Review* (Vol. CXXVI, No. 3).

Characters:
Two play every role here: an actor around 40 to play Dan most of the time, and an actor around 60 to mostly play Paul.

The younger actor has the first line of the play and with each new character-heading they alternate.

Place & Time:
Vancouver, Santa Monica, Syria, Hollywood; 2016-17.

Notes:
The right-hand column of the script contains suggestions of photographs, video, maps, etc., to be projected somewhere prominent onstage, as well as suggestions of light and sound. All of the photographs and video listed are by Paul Watson, except where noted.

Running time is approximately 90-100 minutes without an intermission.

The set is an interpretation of the 2017 viral photo by Joseph Eid of Mohammed Mohiedin Anis listening to music in the wreckage of his bedroom in Aleppo.

New Life was commissioned and developed by Center Theatre Group in Los Angeles, and supported by a Guggenheim Fellowship in Drama & Performance Art.

New Life has received development with the New Harmony Project, the LA Writers' Workshop Festival at Center Theatre Group, and PlayLabs at The Playwrights' Center.

New Life was excerpted with the title "Long Days" in the *Sewanee Review* (Vol. CXXVI, No. 3).

Characters:
Two play every role here: an actor around 40 to play Dan most of the time, and an actor around 60 to mostly play Paul.

The younger actor has the first line of the play and with each new character-heading they alternate.

Place & Time:
Vancouver, Santa Monica, Syria, Hollywood; 2016-17.

Notes:
The right-hand column of the script contains suggestions of photographs, video, maps, etc., to be projected somewhere prominent onstage, as well as suggestions of light and sound. All of the photographs and video listed are by Paul Watson, except where noted.

Running time is approximately 90-100 minutes without an intermission.

The set is an interpretation of the 2017 viral photo by Joseph Eid of Mohammed Mohiedin Anis listening to music in the wreckage of his bedroom in Aleppo.

For Jessica and Bebe, for our new life

Nobody knows anything.

—Ancient Hollywood proverb

1: PREVIOUSLY ON

DAN: Why do I write you? —Why do you write back   *Two voices*
to me?   *in the dark.*

PAUL: How can you believe we're the same,
Dan? when everything's been going your way,
relatively.

DAN: Why are we friends then still,
Paul?

PAUL: You won't leave me in peace, and I don't
deserve to be.   *The sound*

DAN: —The soldier's legs dangled   *of helicopters*
from the doorsill. The belly of the bird   *far off.*
was charcoal—

PAUL: When a shoulder-launched grenade
mangles the gearbox, screwing the Black Hawk
down into Mogadishu.

DAN: That's the shot   *Paul Watson's*
that won you the Pulitzer.   *Pulitzer Prize*

PAUL: Look at it   *-winning photograph.*
at your leisure.

DAN: She's kicking him. Laughing.

PAUL: The world has found its frame.   *The noise of*

DAN: And you're looking   *ithe mob.*
at yourself.

PAUL: And we are violating
whatever made us human.

DAN: —When you hear   *Silence.*
the dead soldier's voice as clear as my voice
warning:

PAUL: If you do this I will own you
forever.

DAN: Forgive me,

PAUL: just understand
I don't want to do this.

DAN: No.

PAUL: We have to
do this.

DAN: Yes.

PAUL: We have to do this until   *The photograph*

we don't.   *disappears*
for now.

2: ELSEWHERE IN THE MEANTIME

VOICE: Name and date of birth please?   *Still dark.*

PAUL: What do you say,
my friend? All that's required is your passport   *An explosion*
and visa. And the airfare. To Kabul   *far off.*
if Kandahar's too far. You can purchase
your tickets online. Pick a window seat
if you're like me, a voyeur. But steer clear   *Slow*
of Afghan Air: holes in the fuselage   *dawn.*
can really bring you down. Try to connect
by way of Dubai instead of Lahore
if you want to avoid getting kidnapped
outside Duty Free. Ha ha ha.

DAN: Dear Paul,
I'm in New York City interviewing
a UN speechwriter in a cafe
on Second Avenue. Due diligence
for our upcoming trip. The speechwriter
is an old friend of mine, an aspiring
playwright, once.

SPEECH: If you put me in your play,
Dan, I hope you'll describe me as a man
often mistaken for Daniel Craig. Or
a Justin Theroux type maybe? —Which one's
your preference?

DAN: While the East River's snaking
between buildings and over his shoulders
like a boa constrictor, I flash back
to 2001, breathing in the stench
of flesh and bone as I jogged past Bellevue
in that Indian summer dusk.

SPEECH: —Advice
about Afghanistan? —Don't go! I mean,
why *would* you?

DAN: Ha ha ha!

PAUL: The best hotels
are colonial. Kevlar vests laid out
like terrycloth robes, helmets like roses
or chocolates on pillows. A cellar full
of bad wine. Wicker chairs, decorative

1: PREVIOUSLY ON

DAN: Why do I write you? —Why do you write back   *Two voices*
           to me?   *in the dark.*

PAUL: How can you believe we're the same,
           Dan? when everything's been going your way,
           relatively.

DAN: Why are we friends then still,
           Paul?

PAUL: You won't leave me in peace, and I don't
           deserve to be.   *The sound*

DAN: —The soldier's legs dangled   *of helicopters*
           from the doorsill. The belly of the bird   *far off.*
           was charcoal—

PAUL: When a shoulder-launched grenade
           mangles the gearbox, screwing the Black Hawk
           down into Mogadishu.

DAN: That's the shot   *Paul Watson's*
           that won you the Pulitzer.   *Pulitzer Prize*

PAUL: Look at it   *-winning photograph.*
           at your leisure.

DAN: She's kicking him. Laughing.

PAUL: The world has found its frame.   *The noise of*

DAN: And you're looking   *ithe mob.*
           at yourself.

PAUL: And we are violating
           whatever made us human.

DAN: —When you hear   *Silence.*
           the dead soldier's voice as clear as my voice
           warning:

PAUL: If you do this I will own you
           forever.

DAN: Forgive me,

PAUL: just understand
           I don't want to do this.

DAN: No.

PAUL: We have to
           do this.

DAN: Yes.

PAUL: We have to do this until   *The photograph*

165

we don't.   *disappears*
                                                              for now.

2: ELSEWHERE IN THE MEANTIME

VOICE: Name and date of birth please?   *Still dark.*
PAUL: What do you say,
                my friend? All that's required is your passport   *An explosion*
                and visa. And the airfare. To Kabul   *far off.*
                if Kandahar's too far. You can purchase
                your tickets online. Pick a window seat
                if you're like me, a voyeur. But steer clear   *Slow*
                of Afghan Air: holes in the fuselage   *dawn.*
                can really bring you down. Try to connect
                by way of Dubai instead of Lahore
                if you want to avoid getting kidnapped
                outside Duty Free. Ha ha ha.
DAN: Dear Paul,
                I'm in New York City interviewing
                a UN speechwriter in a cafe
                on Second Avenue. Due diligence
                for our upcoming trip. The speechwriter
                is an old friend of mine, an aspiring
                playwright, once.
SPEECH: If you put me in your play,
                Dan, I hope you'll describe me as a man
                often mistaken for Daniel Craig. Or
                a Justin Theroux type maybe? —Which one's
                your preference?
DAN: While the East River's snaking
                between buildings and over his shoulders
                like a boa constrictor, I flash back
                to 2001, breathing in the stench
                of flesh and bone as I jogged past Bellevue
                in that Indian summer dusk.
SPEECH: —Advice
                about Afghanistan? —Don't go! I mean,
                why *would* you?
DAN: Ha ha ha!
PAUL: The best hotels
                are colonial. Kevlar vests laid out
                like terrycloth robes, helmets like roses
                or chocolates on pillows. A cellar full
                of bad wine. Wicker chairs, decorative

grasses between us, ceiling fans ticking
like history. Interviewing Najib
for our new play. —You do want to do this,
Dan, right? It's not going to be as easy
as the Arctic was all those years ago
when we first rendezvoused.

VOICE: What's your name, ma'am?
VOICE: Name and date of birth, ma'am?
DAN: The breaking news,   *An explosion*
          Paul, is my wife's got cancer. Breast cancer,   *far off.*
          not early stage, not late. You'll be okay,
          they tell us. One of the more treatable
          cancers. Nobody would sign up for this,
          of course. They say. I'd wandered groggily
          into our sun-drenched kitchen the morning
          of September 11th—of all days
          —and she said, Hey, feel this lump. I couldn't
          do it. I simply said, Oh no, oh no,
          oh no. And sat down. So in other words
          I don't think a trip to Kabul makes sense
          right now.

PAUL: Dear Dan. I don't know what to say.
          What a horror. How can I be of help
          from afar? Just give us a shout. Forget
          about Kabul. Everybody else has
          anyway. And my old fixer Najib
          won't answer my emails. Maybe he's fled
          to Pakistan? or had his tongue cut out
          for working for me. Onward and upward,
          my confessor. I will keep your family
          in my thoughts and prayers. We'll find our new play
          elsewhere in the meantime.

DAN: My wife is tired   *An explosion*
          from the double mastectomy. The breast   *closer.*
          reconstruction. Chemotherapy. Hair
          snowballs in the soft bristles of her brush,
          though she won't go bald. She freezes her scalp
          during infusions. Wears like this helmet?
          made of ice packs that have to be swapped out
          every twenty-two minutes precisely.
          Ice mittens and ice slippers to preserve
          her nails. Ice mask for eyebrows and lashes.
          Mummified. It's all the rage and almost
          de rigueur here in Hollywood. I write
          minimalist poems to her on my phone,

email them to myself. For a future
collection. Of course I worry about
tomorrow. About money. Our daughter
just turned two years old. Would I have to teach
composition somewhere in Missouri,
some miserable widower? —God forbid,
would I have to write for TV? The stress
is taking its toll. I've been having these
awful cramps. Have they sent you somewhere yet,
Paul?

PAUL: Dear Dan, you can watch it happening
in newsrooms all over the world: where once
there'd been like these frenzies of reporters
in vast, cacophonous pens, now you see
coffee-stained carpets and huddled masses
of mourners bidding farewells to colleagues
quitting or fired. Janitors dollying
desks down stairs. Clunk, clunk, clunk. Gone are the shouts
of, you know—Stop the presses! and all that
golden-age jazz now trickling to tapping
fingers on smartphones. —So no. Still waiting
here at home. How are you holding up?

VOICE: Name—
VOICE: Your name please.   *Explosion*
DAN: —*My* name?   *closer.*
VOICE: Date of birth—
DAN: Dear Paul,
the strangest thing has happened. Only months
after my wife—six months that have felt like
a stabbing in slow motion, the knife slash
-ing us both incrementally although
she's doing well—I have been diagnosed
with cancer. Colon. With metastasis
to the liver. They say it's treatable,
even curable, and they use that word,
but nobody mentions survival rates
and I'm too scared to ask. Ten years ago
I would've been given six months to live,
they tell us. My wife and I are shell shocked
again. Why me? I ran. Shopped at Whole Foods.
Bought organically at farmers markets.
I've been a dedicated hand washer
all my life. Didn't smoke. Drank too much sure,
but I'm a writer. Was I too moody,
pessimistic? On the surface maybe

but would I have written a single word
without some form of hope? And stress—who's not
stressed? —And how should we *define* stress? the stress
of publishing a poem? of workshopping
a new play? These things don't count. Did I write
too much about ghosts? Did I call the dead
toward me somehow, naively? writing
too autobiographically? draining
the life out of me somehow? Did we fight
too much, my wife and I, about nothing
that ever really mattered much? Was it
bad feng shui? Pent-up Qi? Was it eating
white flour? corn syrup? gluten? —Monsanto?
Or like that old guy in *The Graduate*
says: One word, plastics. Was it the iPhone
in my back pocket? Not enough flossing?
That year we lived in northern New Jersey?
A slightly embarrassing affection
for Thomas Hardy? The asbestos pipes
in my childhood basement? —If anything's
going to poison me it would have to be
my troubled childhood. Every doctor asks,
Do you have a family history? Oh no,
I answer. Though my wife's quick to explain
we haven't had contact with my family
in a decade or so, and nobody
ever really talked about anything
true anyway. Or went to the doctor
like *ever*. Didn't trust them. My mother
would often say she didn't want to know.
The cure is worse than the sickness, she'd say.
Her philosophy about life, really.
And somehow they've been lucky, still alive,
the latest I've heard. —Could this be the curse
my family placed on me, for leaving them
behind? It's one of the Ten Commandments,
if I remember: Obey thy family,
some bullshit like that. Did I smite myself
out of guilt? because I felt too happy
without my old family? or too happy
with my new? Had I become too happy
all around, finally? —And what *about*
9/11? My future wife's sublet
was saturated in that film of dust
from the twin towers, so the EPA

sends this kid with a vacuum who tells us,
No big deal. Though I'd get like these sore throats
whenever I spent the night. My wife said
I was a hypochondriac. I am
a hypochondriac, but we sometimes
have a point. So I nagged until she moved
a few months later. —Or did this begin
even longer ago? Was the tumor
growing since I was twelve and decided
to become a writer? a suffering,
highly principled, starving artist kind
of writer? Did I believe I believed
in the transcendent power of theatre
while instead shellacking my resentments
into this black pearl of a tumor? —Paul,
did this happen because I emailed you
what, almost ten years ago? I'm ashamed
to say this. But by writing about you,   *Far off,*
did I somehow become an accomplice   *the noise of*
in the desecration of that soldier   *the mob.*
in the streets of Mogadishu? You win
a Pulitzer. My play about you wins   *Helicopters.*
a Guggenheim. You heard the dead man speak
both in your head and out: *If you do this*
I will own you forever. Does he mean
me, too? Is this the sinful thing I've done
that deserves such punishment? One doctor
advised: Don't ask, Why me? —Why *not* you? Why
not any of us? —All that's to say, Paul,
Friday they'll resection my colon. Then
chemo. Then they'll resection my liver.
Then more chemo. I'll be done by Christmas.
Doesn't mean we're not going to write this play,
but I'm having a hard time believing
anything I could write could matter now.
This isn't despair. Another doctor
asked me if I've been having any thoughts
of suicide. And I laughed. I simply
want to live. I want more life. I don't want
to finish anything. Apologies
for such a long email. We'll know much more
after surgery. Put in a good word
with a few of those Inuit shamans
you know.

PAUL: Dear Dan, when I wrote thoughts and prayers

I was half-lying. Though I do believe
in ghosts. As you know. Go figure. So yes
to shamanic intervention. I've sent
requests as far afield as Grise Fiord. Here
is a video of the northern lights
over Iqaluit in Nunavut.   *The shimmering*
Because I know someday we'll be able   *suggestion of the*
to watch this show together, side by side   *greens and violets*
upon the crackling shelf of pack ice   *of the northern*
without the intrusion of manmade light,   *lights.*
while camping in our igloo. Until then,
my friend, if you can, find a quiet place
inside your own mind if nowhere else and
let the spirits help. I think about you
ceaselessly—sleeplessly so. I believe
you will get better because you are strong
and the spirits know we need you. You are
a healer, I know this firsthand. You will
heal yourself. No doubt you will be facing
things only you can tell, with your own words.
So have no fear, my friend. We have more tales
to tell, you and me.

DAN: Are you still waiting
at home, Paul?

PAUL: I'm expecting to depart
after my new body armor arrives
from Dallas. It's on backorder after
that most recent culling of schoolchildren
in your country, Dan. We get so angry
at presidents and politicians when
what we ought to do is just pause and check
the courage of our own convictions. Well,
I've checked mine, and it's my wife and my son
who are courageous. I think I may die
in Syria. Truly, Dan. I've survived
so many times before and I don't know
why. But this is different, I can feel it.
And when I'm gone, editors and anchors
claiming to know me will offer up self
-serving sound bites. —But you actually *do*
know me, my friend. I'll tell my wife to send
all inquiries your way.

DAN: Where are you now?
PAUL: Standing on a balcony with a view
of the Mediterranean. Sunset.   *The sound*

Sipping scotch. My son has become a teen   *of waves.*
somehow. Hemingway's the cat. He's puking
again. We're FaceTiming: "Where are you now,
Dad?" Beirut. Tonight. "Where are you going?"
Syria. Just a few weeks. I'll be home
before you know it. "Why do you have to?"
It's my job. "You don't have to, you could just
stay home." He starts to cry. "I'm going to go
snowboarding," he says. —If I don't come back
alive, Scott, please know: all you'll need to do
is climb up the mountain and ask the trees
whether to ask out that girl. Ask the rain
how to handle your mother. Ask the storm
to borrow His car.

DAN: What does your son say
to all that, Paul?

PAUL: Nothing. I can't say this
to him. In reality.

DAN: Ha ha ha.

PAUL: I was complaining again to my wife
the other night and she suddenly asked,
Why can't you just stop? No more war. What then?
And I told her I'd fly to Hollywood
to pitch a TV series *about* war
with Dan. I know you're busy. But maybe
you'd like the distraction?

DAN: This is my name.
This is my date of birth.

NURSE: Here's your wristband.
Here's your gown. Here's the gas. Try to relax
and breathe in.

DAN: Breathe in. Breathe in.

PAUL: As always
I'll be your eyes and ears and you can be
my voice. One more time. So what do you say,
my friend? The plan is I'll reach Aleppo
tomorrow. And I'm hoping to come back
with some killer, high-concept anecdotes
sure to cinch our pitch.

3: DISPATCHES

"I'm talking to you!" Outside the restaurant
Al-Quds, Arabic for Jerusalem
for some reason. Bat-like chickens roasting
in respiring flames. For broken spirits
without power. The constant thump and crash
of mortar blast. A canopy of stars.
"Whenever we see Americans—that's when
Bashar bombs us!" Everybody's laughing
at me. I tell them I'm Canadian.
The man at the door gives me a chicken
wrapped in wax paper. —Shukran! Then ducking   *An explosion.*
into this maternity clinic where
I'm sleeping tonight. A doctor suggests
the basement. I tell him not to worry,
we have a saying in Canadian:
Lightning never strikes twice. —Just then the door's   *Loud explosion.*
kicked open and barking men deliver
the contorting, shouting, weeping heap of
the man who gave me chicken. His bare feet
are dripping blood. In the flickering light   *This video silently,*
nobody notices me recording   *briefly.*
over their shoulders, between their heads, blood
on linoleum, snailed ointment tubes, husks
of gauze wrappers. "Hold him still." A male nurse
in a pink-collared sweater is swaddling
the chicken man from heel to toe. —Dear Dan:
I'd like to remind my readers back home
to listen. But I was the one hungry
for chicken. Which is why I missed the point
of a joke told in the dark.

DAN: I wake up
from the anesthesia to discover
my gut stapled from pubis to navel.
The tumor was as big as a softball,
they say. But at least nobody employs
a fruit simile. They had to slice out
six inches of my descending colon,
stitch the ends back together. Had to nick
some of my bladder too, just to be safe.
At first I'm conscious of every breath like—
NURSE: Now take a deep breath. Now take a few steps.
DAN: —a cool drink of water. When I attempt
to take those few steps, I literally swoon

into the arms of a male nurse, who feels
my forehead with his forearm. Like a frieze
of the passion. If you will. Three days pass
until they suggest—

NURSE: Here, take a few sips.
DAN: But something's wrong, I start throwing up this
black bile, spike a fever of a hundred
and five. Maybe it was the Dilaudid
but every time I close my eyes I see
people at my bedside.

PEOPLE: Hello.
DAN: People
not actually there.

PEOPLE: What's your name?
DAN: Strangers
and my parents. —I didn't want to see
my parents.

MY MOTHER: Where have you been, Danny? Why
won't you call?

DAN: I'd begged my wife to make sure
my name had been left off the registry
but I needn't have worried. No family
shows up, calls, emails, texts. As you know, Paul,
the gravely ill will often call out for
their mothers, which only seems natural.
But I don't. I can't. —Opening my eyes
on the hospital. Closing them again
I see travelers whirling about like
Grand Central. Like souls slipping down the banks
of the River Styx. Some are stopping now
to notice me. They shove a tube into
my nose—

NURSE: Hold still.
DAN: —down into my stomach
to drain the bile. Gagging—

NURSE: Hold him.
DAN: —struggling
in their arms.

NURSE: Breathe in.
DAN: The surgeon arrives
munching on a Kind Bar. The surgeon's name
sounds alarmingly like Kevorkian.
He's inclined to cut.

KASANJIAN: It's a tossup though,
DAN: he says. —Maybe I just need some more time

                                        to heal?
KASANJIAN: Your call.
DAN: I get lucky. Daily
                        my wife leads me shuffling through the halls
                        of the hospital, my ass winking out
                        of my gown, pushing my tree of IVs,
                        piss-bag dangling too, taking in the views
                        of the frat houses of UCLA,
                        cars, palm trees, celluloid sun. Good Friday
                        when I was admitted. Which is good news
                        from a certain point of view. Thirteen days
                        in the hospital. My lucky number,
                        I've always believed. Because that's the day,
                        February 13th, when my brother
                        jumps out the window of our attic when
                        he was seventeen and I was twelve and
                        somehow he's still alive. And I'm home. Home   *Sun.*
                        now, Paul, with my wife and daughter, who asks
                        after the status of my mysterious
                        booboo. The lumen port bulges my arm
                        like a medieval bubo. Catheter
                        up my dingus still, bag strapped to my thigh,
                        tube draining puss and urine from my side
                        into a squeeze bulb, and of course there's that
                        slasher-film scar. Or maybe it's more like
                        a vertical C-section. Will it heal
                        away? my daughter asks. Away, away,
                        she used to sing as a baby pointing
                        at the moon as we strolled.
PAUL: A young man stops
                        an old man. The old man has been nosing   *Photos*
                        his motorbike through rubble with a boy   *of some of this.*
                        in his lap. The nervous old man's grinning
                        like Arafat. The boy's knuckles dimple
                        as he gingerly accepts the assault
                        rifle from our rebel. —Who'd earlier   *This photo.*
                        unbuttoned his shirt to display three scars
                        like pink planets curving from his belly
                        to his breast. "Friend," he said, "touch." So I touched
                        his wounds. And took this picture. While his breath
                        lifted in veils. He told me a bullet
                        sleeps beside his heart. He told his doctor:
                        "Leave it for Allah and let me go back
                        to war." —Back in the present tense our boy   *Back to*
                        is giggling like a boy. Slender fingers   *this photo*

tickling the trigger. The rebel's pinching   *again.*
the muzzle into a sullen sky while
his free fingers resemble a peace sign
mistakenly, I'm sure. "Take the shot now,"
he says, "friend." —This penniless young man   *Camera click, this*
is not afraid to die. Like Lazarus   *photo's gone.*
unwinding his winding sheet in pursuit
of fleeing loyalists. His headband stitched
with Arabic creeds. Rings on his fingers   *A selection*
like a magician. Pinging city streets   *of these photos*
with "Allahu akbar!" before hammering   *now.*
bullets around corners. Sniper curtains
have been shot to bits—so we run for it
across the avenue. Then hands on knees
laughing in the alleyway. Laddering
into our own sniper's nest. Candle stub
guttering as twilight falls. "Men are born
to die in war." I ask him to tell me
what his tattoos mean. "This one is a poem
to my brother," he says. The Shabiha
captured him. Cut off his penis. Beat him
with pipes, shocked him with wires. Starved him until
he was just a wisp of flame to be snuffed
by the wind. Then dumped him into a hole
with rats and snow. I ask, "And what about
this tattoo here?" He tells me these words mean
there is no one left to trust. No family,
no friends. Smiling as he hands me his flask
of milk tea. Says he's not the same man as   *This picture:*
the man he hates.   *briefly.*

DAN: The chemotherapy
makes my eyes ache when I cry. When I eat
my salivary glands ache. My fingers
trembling as I type. —I don't think I can
keep writing about you, Paul. The cancer
was growing in me while I wrote that play
about your life. Your life makes me gag now,
though that could be just the chemo. Maybe
the things you've witnessed should've sickened me
all along? Maybe my mother was right
to criticize what I wrote as a boy
as being too dark, too depressing. Now
all I want is to run as far away   *The sound*
as I can from the truth—   *of a helicopter*

PAUL: Death's a spider   *high above.*

spinning overhead, dangling its dread sac
of water heaters, gas canisters or
rusted mufflers with stabilizing fins
soldered on—basically pieces-of-shit
IEDs of TNT, nitrogen
-rich fertilizer, diesel, anything
meant to keep burning after exploding
upon impact. Scrap metal for shrapnel
like candy inside piñatas. Released
into their toppling, almost human
-like spiraling, like sky-diving lovers
flailing and clutching, until they align
in a bullet-nosed dive into the hum
-drum day below. Light, sound. The mushroom cloud   *Light, sound.*
drifts. The smog of plastic burning, snow drifts
of concrete. —Then voices crying "Help me,
Mama!" beneath new earth. Survivors look
like stereotyped Africans wearing
masks of white ash. Or debauched characters
in some sick comedy of manners. Limbs
like tangled marionettes. An old man blinks
pantsless on his toilet in what had been
his bathroom. Then bits of spine, bits of spine
tossed on a blanket. A woman's bare foot
sticks out of the mountain. They tickle her
to see if they should dig. We hear her voice:
"My legs! —Where are my legs!" The digging man
looks into my camera: "We come for you,"
he says. By which he means Bashar and not
the buried woman.

DAN: I tried to heal you,
Paul, and I believed that telling the truth
about you, about what you've seen—somehow
I'd be healed too. But my faith's been shaken.
—Or is this the point? Do not look away
now. Especially now.

PAUL: A teenaged girl
looks up at a mountain of rubble. Mouth
hangs open. As if she's impressed. Wire mesh
in broken concrete like the antennae
of gigantic roaches. Squashed. Beneath stairs
cascading sideways. Neighbors spin their lives
out of bedrooms cut in half. All these stones
as if the world's walls have been dismantled
and cascaded over Homs.

DAN: Be my eyes,
Paul.   Let me still be your voice.
PAUL: But my eyes
         adore the girl's clean-eyed stare. Like, Nothing   *This photo.*
         here worth noting. Or looting. She pivots
         on her heel. Runs off. As a teenaged boy
         strides past flipping his hood up to the rain.
         He looks at me. Then up at the mountain   *All this destruction*
         of nothing. To see what I see. Nothing   *transforming*
         worth noting, or looting. Walk on.   *into:*

4: SALVAGING   *A living room*
                                                           in a house in
DAN: Wow.   *Vancouver with*
PAUL: There's a steam room too. You look surprised.
         This isn't me, it's Zelda. Zelda, Dan.   *walls of windows*
         Dan, Zelda.   *looking out on*
DAN: Nice to finally meet you,   *brooding green.*
         Zelda.
PAUL: She's shy.   *Rain storm*
DAN: Okay. —Bye.   *clearing away,*
PAUL: She's busy
         making us dinner. Let me take your coat   *sun setting.*
         and your bag.
DAN: So your wife is named Zelda
         and your son is Scott?
PAUL: Zelda chose the name
         while she was pregnant and watching TV
         in Vienna. I was holed up somewhere
         in the Balkans. And she saw the name Scott
         rolling up the screen, like in the credits,
         and she liked the look of it. I said fine,
         but not without first explaining to her
         that F. Scott and Zelda Fitzgerald were
         both bat-shit insane.
DAN: Ha ha ha.
PAUL: —So what,
         the government just gives you money?
DAN: What?
PAUL: —For this trip!
DAN: Well the grant was for Kabul,
         but once you tell people you've got cancer
         they tend to just let things slide.

PAUL: How are you?
You look good—no, you do! You look almost
healthy?

DAN: I call it the chemo diet.

PAUL: —Ha ha ha!

DAN: It's the second week after
infusion, which is like I mentioned when
I can feel sort of okay. Still tired. Still
queasy.

PAUL: Are you going to puke?

DAN: What—now? No.

PAUL: You sure?

DAN: Things taste bad. My taste buds are shot.
And the smell—everything smells like chemo,
you know?

PAUL: And what does that smell like.

DAN: Garbage.
And flowers. Oddly. So flowers smell like
garbage now. Which is too bad. But so far
no, no puking. They give me pills for that
anyway. Which leaves you constipated,
but you pick your battles.

PAUL: I got to say,
at first I thought: this is bad news. You know?
He's not going to make it. I told Zelda,
That's it. Curtains.

DAN: Well you could've fooled me,
I mean—what you wrote.

PAUL: You know how it is.
You can't tell the truth. —But you look really,
really good! Have a seat.

DAN: Here?

PAUL: And you're not
bald.

DAN: Oh. —No.

PAUL: I'm relieved. I was prepping
for baldness.

DAN: Well, my particular drugs
just thin the hair. And make the follicles
feel almost plastic? My father was bald
and I hated him, so I'm glad. —My skin's
as soft as a baby's—

PAUL: Oh yeah?

DAN: Touch it.

PAUL: Really?

DAN: Touch! —Touch!
PAUL: It *is* soft.
DAN: Ha ha ha.
PAUL: —And no—what's it—?
DAN: Colostomy bag. Nope.
PAUL: That's good.
DAN: —You're telling me.
PAUL: Hey, want to play
       some music? I'm thinking we could use this   *Tom Waits's*
       as our theme song—   *"Day After*
DAN: Well let's sell our pitch first—   *Tomorrow."*
PAUL: With like a montage during the credits
       of real combat journalists, some living,
       some dead—giving our show an American
       brand of hauntedness. You know what I mean
       by hauntedness? You want a drink?
DAN: I can't,
       my liver.
PAUL: What about the medical
       oobie doobage?
DAN: Turns out marijuana
       freaks me out. When I was recovering
       from surgery, I stupidly swallowed
       a whole dropper full of THC oil
       and started losing my mind—
PAUL: Ha ha ha—
DAN: All I wanted was like to tear the tubes
       out of my body and run stark naked
       through the neighborhood screaming—
PAUL: Ha ha ha!
DAN: Don't you see what's happening? Don't you see
       I may be dying up here in this room?
       With the sunlight in the venetian blinds.
       I couldn't sleep for days. I speedball now
       with coffee and Ativan.
PAUL: Mind if I
       partake?
DAN: Be my guest.
PAUL: Man, I love Tom Waits.
       This is my favorite part: How does God choose?
       Whose prayers does he refuse? Who turns the wheel?
       Who throws the dice? Oh-on the day after
       tomor-or-ow?
DAN: That's nice.
PAUL: It's like we're back

                              in the Arctic again. How many years
                              has it been?
DAN: I don't want to count.
PAUL: Jesus.
                              How did that Inuit elder put it?
                              The earth is moving faster now. He meant
                              global warming, but still. Have I told you
                              I'm heading north again? for a feature
                              about the lost Franklin Expedition.
DAN: —You're kidding me. —I'm obsessed with Franklin.
                              How they just disappeared. Leaving behind
                              silverware and tuxedoes on the ice,
                              a few corpses in cairns.
PAUL: There's a story
                              still told by the shamans, of paddling by
                              these two ghost ships ensnared in floating floes.
                              And how they climbed aboard and down below
                              found piles of frozen bodies, including
                              Lord Franklin himself. Though he was sitting
                              upright in his chair. A bald and stout man
                              with mutton chops. Big grinning yellow teeth
                              like tusks. It's called the scurvy smile because
                              your gums shrink.
DAN: Ha ha ha.
PAUL: Off the record,
                              they're going to find those ships any day now:
                              Erebus, christened for the nether realm
                              the dead pass through on their way to Hades,
                              and the *Terror*. Names that were just asking
                              for trouble, if you ask me.
DAN: Ha ha ha.
PAUL: —After a hundred and seventy years
                              frozen in the ever-loving ice!
DAN: —Hey
                              maybe I'll apply for another grant
                              to go with you?
PAUL: —I'd love that!
DAN: Do you mind
                              if I record this? for our pitch?
PAUL: What's wrong?
DAN: I can't find my phone.
PAUL: Maybe you left it
                              in the cab?
DAN: Shit—
PAUL: Because I'm forgetting

everything these days. Except everything
I can't. Those kids in Aleppo salvaged
from landslides of buildings. Some are shrieking
like they're being born again. I think, How
can *I* help?

DAN: And I remember the hand   *Andrew Stawicki's*
Paul was born without, the opposable   *photo of Paul*
nub of a thumb at the end of his arm   *taking a photo in*
like an elephant's trunk.   *Sudan in the nineties:*

PAUL: I need new shoes
that can weather these winters. Do these jeans   *Paul's handless arm*
make me look fat?   *is prominent.*

DAN: his boyish helplessness
that disarms. If you will.

PAUL: Zelda's broiling
prawns. —You like prawns?

DAN: Which is precisely when
he tends to let slip his anecdotes like
they're meaningless.

PAUL: Like I was saying to
my interpreter outside this café
in Aleppo: Every revolution
has a problem with power. Submitting
Iraq as an example. Jihadis
come with strings attached. Beheadings, stonings,
prepubescent girls raped in the name of
Allah. Surely you haven't risen up
against a millennia of tyrants
just to pimp your children to *these* psychos
instead? —A young man rose up: "Your country
did nothing." Pointing at me. I feel like
he's going to slap my face. "America watched
and did nothing." Have I betrayed this man
personally? "The blood of our children
stains your hands." Trying to smooth things over,
an old man interjects: "We do not love
ISIS. But the more our families are killed
by the pig Bashar, the more we will learn
to love." —Maybe we can find a way, Dan,
to work this into our pitch?

DAN: —But tell me,
Paul, what could we possibly be doing
differently there? If we've learned anything
from the last fifteen years it's that we should
spend more time at home.

PAUL: Anything's better
than nothing.

DAN: Is it?

PAUL: The west engages
in these self-soothing debates, with Assad
toppling town after town, tilting the board
in Putin's favor. Turkey too. I wish
I were your age! And childless. With two hands
for my Kalashnikov. But I suppose
we'll have to take our fight to Hollywood
instead. Am I right, Dan? Speaking of which,
you're sure we're going to be able to pitch
this summer? I'll try to keep the hounds fed
till then. —I've got a few good examples   *Evening.*
of realistic dialogue,

DAN: offers Paul
that evening after dinner with Zelda,
while Scott does his homework upstairs.

PAUL: Take this
al-Nusra rebel, who was not inclined
to get his picture taken. So I aim
at his feet for that cliché of a doll
in a puddle of blood. —Why are you here?
he spits at me. I tell him: Do your job,
tough guy, and I'll do mine. —Do you like that?

DAN: Like it how?

PAUL: For our script.

DAN: Don't you worry
about traveling with the rebels? I mean,
they may not be ISIS but they commit
war crimes too.

PAUL: Everybody's committing
war crimes. *We* are. I was having dinner
in Turkey with a bunch of reporters
talking about that YouTube video,
I'm sure you've seen—of an Assad soldier
buried up to his chin, gulping for air,
there's jeering and shovels showering him
with dirt. And then US-backed jackboots
stamp out his cries.

DAN: We can't be neutral though,
can we? This could be the Achilles' heel
of our pitch, to be honest. We need clear
villains and heroes—

ZELDA: Do you both believe

you can sell this?

DAN: Zelda speaks.

PAUL: Zelda speaks
her mind, Dan. When she speaks. You've been warned.

DAN: Well,
I believe we have a chance to sell it.
Don't you, Paul?

ZELDA: American television
is evil.

DAN: Sure, but—

PAUL: Dan's wife's on TV—

DAN: Sometimes.

PAUL: Full disclosure.

DAN: She wrote a show
and co-starred in it. It has a real cult
following.

ZELDA: And does your wife support you?

DAN: What—financially?

PAUL: Zelda.

DAN: She earns more
than me. Does Paul earn more than you?

PAUL: —Dan's wife
is the reason we have a producer
setting this thing up.

DAN: Ari.

ZELDA: Sounds Jewish.

DAN: Well—he is. Half Jewish. His grandfather
invented backyard pools.

ZELDA: Well that's something.

DAN: He's a good producer.

PAUL: There's good TV
and there's bad TV, Zelda—

DAN: We're aiming
for the first—

ZELDA: Americans are stupid though.

DAN: Okay—I'm American—

ZELDA: So's Donald Trump.

DAN: Trump's going to get impeached. Or be voted
out of office.

ZELDA: —What is he? Honestly.
A professional wrestler?

DAN: Ha ha ha.

ZELDA: A Russian asset? A cokehead? Late-stage
syphilis? He's like something vomited
up from the bowels of the American

subconscious—

DAN: Well I didn't vote for him—

ZELDA: But many did. Do you know why? Because
he tells stories. Popular. Involving
the Other: the Chinese, the Mexicans,
the Muslims. And the Blacks in your country.
He understands that white people want walls
around everything. Themselves. Wait and see,
he will win again. Trump knows how to sell
stupid stories.

DAN: Ha ha ha.

ZELDA: So will you
make Syria stupid?

DAN: Our plan is to
reach people.

PAUL: That's right, Zelda.

DAN: As many
as possible. That's why we're creating
a TV show and not another play.

ZELDA: But I thought that play you wrote about Paul
was successful?

DAN: It was. But not many
people saw it.

ZELDA: Does that matter? Numbers?

DAN: Maybe. I guess.

ZELDA: So you're selling out then.

DAN: If you mean trying to reach people with
the truth—

PAUL: It's about journalism too,
Zelda.

DAN: About precisely the problem
of telling the story of Syria
to a world that doesn't care.

ZELDA: Well good luck
with all that.

DAN: You think we're wasting our time.

ZELDA: —Paul, put your phone away. —What's wrong?

DAN: Hey Paul—

PAUL: Just an email. An old friend.

DAN: —You don't think
our pitch is a waste of time, do you, Paul?

PAUL: I've got to go—get another bottle
from downstairs. Be right back.

DAN: Obviously,
Zelda, Paul wants to do this. And I hope

I'm not, you know, out of bounds to assume
you want that too. Writing a TV show
is how he might be able to retire
from war reporting while still salvaging
something valuable. —If it's the money
you're worried about—

ZELDA: It's not the money
that worries me.

DAN: And I'm not doing this
for money either—

ZELDA: Because there isn't
any money yet, right? Paul will tell me
I've been rude. You're unwell. Let me finish
the dishes.

DAN: I can help—

PAUL: Ah-h-h-h,   *Late night.*
the suffocating yet cleansing release
of steam.

DAN: Later that night we're relaxing
in Paul's steam room.   *Steam room.*

PAUL: Let me know if you're hot.

DAN: Whew

PAUL: This okay for you? like medically?   *The steam*

DAN: I don't know. We'll see.   *should resemble*

PAUL: I'm going to just go   *the rubble dust*
commando here. You okay with that, Dan?   *of Aleppo or Homs*
We won't be able to see each other
in a minute. Because of all this steam.

DAN: I think I'll just—stay clothed.

PAUL: Another thing
we need to start working into our pitch
is Combat Sex. You know what I mean by
Combat Sex.

DAN: I guess?

PAUL: Like in Kosovo,
the walls of the safe house were rocking like
a honeymoon suite with NATO bombing
us back to the Stone Age. Everybody's
snorting Ritalin and fucking like rabbits
but not me. I'm just sitting there lusting
for Zelda back home. My son Scott was born
within the year.

DAN: That's—something.

PAUL: It's boredom
combined with a fear of imminent death:

it's hot.

DAN: That hasn't been my experience
with cancer.

PAUL: Well maybe cancer and war
aren't the same.

DAN: I know they're not the same.
I hate it when people describe cancer
in terms of war. Battling cancer. Losing
a battle with cancer. As if cancer's
this kind of external adversary
and not their body. As if survivors
fought harder or better or more bravely
or more positively, or fought with God
on their side. If I survive it's because
I get lucky. That's it.

PAUL: That's how I feel
in war zones.

DAN: Are you going to go back to
Syria before our pitch?

PAUL: Time will tell,
it's the insurance again. This new hitch
concerns so-called accidents. I asked them,
Are death by crossfire and beheading both
covered?

DAN: They're not?

PAUL: It's a cost-benefit
thing. You know like: Why do we need to go
now? And if we *do* go now, how will we
find the extra hundred thousand dollars
it'll take to retrieve the headless corpse
of Watson? I feel like I'm arguing
for a spot on Death Row. Though truthfully
I've been wondering lately if your play's
to blame.

DAN: My what? our play? —For what?

PAUL: That play
you wrote about me. Because the bosses
should never know you're human. Though I doubt
my editors have ever even stepped
inside a theatre.

DAN: Look, Paul—I'm sorry
if anything I've written about you
has caused any—

PAUL: No no no you've saved me,
you're my confessor! You're saving me now

just by being here. Planning this. Let me
give you another. I got this email—

DAN: During dinner?

PAUL: That's the one. From Sayed
who's an interpreter I helped escape
from Kandahar. By writing articles
about Sayed. He lives in Edmonton
now. Laminating IDs. The deceased
are Sayed's sister and sister-in-law
and the women's babies. Sayed's brother
Ahmed was driving. A bump in the road
is an IED. He dragged his family   *Bright light*
into the brush. Where they bled out. One son   *in the dust.*
escaped with Ahmed, with a broken leg
that went necrotic. Tubes in wounds. He asked
where his mother was. He wanted to sleep
beside her. He begged his father: "Take me   *Far away*
someplace else. Another blast is coming."   *explosion.*

DAN: That's awful.

PAUL: Because the Taliban work   *Bright light*
from meticulous lists. Like the ancient   *grows.*
Pashtun proverb says: "You have the watches
but we have the time." When I went downstairs
for this bottle before, I called Sayed
and found myself crying when he answered
on the first ring. "Everything that happens,"
he told me, "is God's design. He decides
who lives and who must die." But he regrets
leaving them behind. Says he should've stayed   *The dusty light*
at home to die with them. We are the ones   *now dissipates.*
to blame now. I'd go back but I don't think
I'd be able to face all the faces
of those whose mothers and babies are dead
because I was the one to post their names
online. With pictures. That's why I'm drinking
too much tonight. —You sure—?

DAN: I'm good.

PAUL: Self-harm
gets bandied about with war veterans but
how's this for our pitch: our semi-retired
protagonist, pessimistic, packing
a pistol for protection, against all
sense and precedent, one night he sucks it
in his mouth and—blackout. Sayed's brother   *Far away*
got a phone call. "We are waiting," the voice   *explosion.*

was whispering. "For men like you there is
no forgiveness."

DAN: Did you carry a gun
in Syria, Paul? Do you have a gun
here at home?

PAUL: Sometimes when I'm here at home
I feel like a dead guest on a talk show
with other dead guests and a dead host who
entertain a studio audience
of the dead, all for the invisible
dead who watch at home.

DAN: Are you still there, Paul?
I can hardly see you. We need to get
serious. If we're going to be ready
for Hollywood this summer. This summer.
I have trouble imagining summer.
Time is so slowly moving so quickly.   *The steam*
I'm back at Cedars Sinai and sitting   *clearing.*
in the chemo chair on Tuesday. Every
other Tuesday, mercifully. A Tuesday
on September 11th, the event
that may have caused the cancer, the event
you may have caused, Paul, with your photograph
of that dead soldier in Mogadishu
because it emboldened Al-Qaeda
by your own admission. I can't say this
to your face, of course. Also a Tuesday
in 1986 when my brother
threw himself out the window—that story
I can't stop telling. Also a Tuesday
the day I was born. These chairs feel like seats
on some rocket ship to the afterlife
or to remission. I don't like that word,
remission. Too reminiscent of sin
and inquisition. These treatments are hard
and getting harder. It's cumulative,
the doctors like to say. Sometimes my counts
are too low to play. You know, red and white
blood cells, platelets. So we take a week off
to bounce back—into the chair. Weeks crawl by
when I don't write. Can't. Dare not. Stopped writing
in my journal. My Moleskine. From fatigue
but also because I can't imagine
wanting to remember. I want to sink
into a hole in the ground and wait out

the apocalypse, so to speak. But then
Wednesdays come. A week and a day after
the infusion. I find my legs and climb
out of the chair. Like a bomb-buried man
digging himself out. I begin to feel
like myself again, I begin to feel
optimistic even! I go running
slowly, surely. I find myself wanting
to write! To become a new man. I will
wear bright clothes. Eat more greens. The good news is
recent scans show my two liver lesions
shrinking. They may be dead. I'm rejoicing
and still I'm terrified. I'm terrified
and still I'm filling with joy. Like I'm young
again. You know? Anything can happen,
good or bad. It's up to me. Each moment
I'm alive.

5: COLD OPEN

PAUL: FADE IN on a paraffin lamp, LISPING
             like the tongue of the Deceiver. O/S
             CALL TO PRAYER.   *The Muslim*
DAN: INT. A CLINIC   *call to prayer.*
             – PREDAWN PAUL, 50s, his hoarfrost stubble
             BRUSHING the dust of Aleppo's rubble
             from a blanket.   *Some version*
PAUL: Dan, you up?   *of Paul's earlier*
DAN: You bet, boss.   *photographs*
             Dan's WRESTLING with a contact lens.   *and videos*
PAUL: Let's go   *of Aleppo projected*
             now. Rebels are pulling out and ISIS   *without sound.*
             won't wait.
DAN: JOYCE wakes up. She's twenty-something—
PAUL: Full lips and sultry eyes—
DAN: Peeking over
             a stack of empty flour sacks.
PAUL: SNARLING FLIES
             pester her dewiness, as she NESTLES
             another rubble-infested blanket
             to her PERKY BREASTS.
JOYCE: I burned my burqa
             last night at dusk, sneaked back in here to sleep

with you guys—

PAUL: LAURENT, Frenchman with a prick
-ish grin, a satyr ARCHING his bare back
behind Joyce:

LAURENT: We combat photographers
have to—how you Americans say?—stick it
together! Ha ha ha.

PAUL: Jesus, Joyce, (MORE)
if you don't want your funbags FILLETED
and hanging off a tree, put some clothes on
NOW!

JOYCE: Relax, old man. I'll be in that van
before you are.

PAUL: She's GATHERING cameras
and lingerie,

DAN: Dan can't help but notice
as he fumbles UNPLUGGING his phone.

PAUL: Paul
can't find his PILLS.

LAURENT: To Joyce: Some Combat Sex
would chill that guy out, no?

PAUL: EXT. – KEYS
TAPPING a blood-smeared door. Sirens BLARING
beyond ABDEL, their fixer. —We're ready,
Abdel! Please thank our hosts for us. Make sure
we've paid them enough.

DAN: EXT. OUR GANG   *Sunlight.*
TIPTOEING – MORNING

PAUL: to their Toyota
Sienna. Fire-glazed, spider-webbed windshield,
bullet holes like zebra stripes. IDLING
roadside. Abdel says the rebels are mad.

DAN: At us? Why?

PAUL: They say they can't guarantee
our safe passage. He wants to drive us to
Beirut today.

LAURENT: But stop at Starbuck's first,
Abdel, s'il vous plaît.

PAUL: Poor Abdel's FONDLING
the blood-gold token of the Arabic
Dua e Safar, supplicant totem
for travelers,

DAN: REVOLVING from his rearview
mirror like air freshener, as our van
SKIDS out of the snowbank of concrete dust

into the street.

JOYCE: —Abdel, ease up a bit,
will you?

DAN: Joyce SHOUTS.

PAUL: Abdel appeals MUTELY
to the men whose minds are ELSEWHERE,

DAN: then slows
a hair.

JOYCE: —Shukriya,

DAN: says Joyce.

JOYCE: Shukriya,
Abdel.

DAN: Which means thank you for some reason
in Urdu.

PAUL: The six al-Nusra rebels
who'd been our guides were laid out side by side
in the street. Each of their heads had been cut
clean off. Placed on their shins. Their genitals
removed and stuffed inside their mouths. The throat
of a boy had been slit, blood like a bib
soaked his naked chest. ISIS with long knives
watched us drive past.

DAN: —Did that really happen,
Paul? —Paul?

PAUL: Just write it down.

DAN: Writer scribbling
shakily—

PAUL: EXT. / INT.
Hand-held cam:

DAN: Abdel's pale, sweating.

PAUL: Close up
on Joyce sexily SNAPPING photographs
through her OPEN WINDOW, sweeping jet-black
silken hair behind a SUPPLE ear,

DAN: while
Dan our cub reporter pretends he's not
INHALING HER SCENT.

PAUL: What's-his-name—

DAN: Laurent.

PAUL: —is frowning. Like most French photographers
he scoffs at artists making art en route
and BUZZES HIS WINDOW UP.

DAN: He prefers
to get in the face of war, as strafing
explodes his background.

PAUL: Everybody RIBS
our reluctant Frenchman:
DAN: Safari rules
not good enough for you, Laurent?
PAUL: CRAWLING
through a village,
DAN: barefoot boys hugging walls,
watching the sky, pointing—
PAUL: POV JOYCE
framing a photograph of a woman
swathed in black burqa,
DAN: busy HUSTLING
her baby indoors—
PAUL: Don't like this.
DAN: What's wrong?
PAUL: Where are the men?
DAN: Fighter jets are circling
above us, Paul. —There.
PAUL: Do fighter jets fire
rockets at vans, Abdel?
DAN: Joyce keeps SNAPPING
her pictures.
PAUL: —Faster.
LAURENT: Why don't we just park
and say bonjour?
PAUL: See those burqas, Laurent?
That means ISIS. And warplanes overhead
means Bashar. —Drive faster.
DAN: A hand grenade
squirts through the open window,
PAUL: ricochets
off Joyce's telephoto,
DAN: rebounds off
Laurent's closed window—
PAUL: before settling
in his lap.
LAURENT: Merde.
PAUL: —Instantly he's fumbling
the door open—he's scissoring his boots—
LAURENT: Merde—merde—merde—
PAUL: Halfway out of the car and
into the street
DAN: as if he's a dancer
in some macabre ballet
PAUL: —until the blast

severs his legs at mid-thigh.

DAN: Dust white light—   *White light.*

PAUL: White light and dust drifting—

DAN: As the others
wrestle his body back into the van,

PAUL: as Abdel's PEELING away,

DAN: the RINGING   *Ringing.*
in our audience's ears does not stop
the Americans from clasping the Frenchman
as he bleeds out. We wipe the screen.

PAUL: That night,
returned safely from the border, the young
reporter Dan and photographer Joyce
fuck like rabbits. Stoned on hash, drunk on death
not choosing them.

DAN: Credits roll and our first
commercial break.

6: LONG DAYS

Thank you for these pages, Paul. Normally
pitching is prose. Conversation, really.
But yeah, it sure is fun to imagine.
I had hoped to finish our pitch before
my surgery. Aware anesthesia
carries with it the possibility
of not waking up. Uncontrollable
bleeding. Heart failure, stroke. Clots and sepsis
in the days after. In the days before,
I start anxiously Googling myself
to somehow prove I'm still alive, and find,
instead of my author's photo, Google
provides an image of Kevin Carter,
a white South African war reporter
in the nineties, member of the so-called
Bang Bang Club, who won a Pulitzer Prize
that same year as you, who haunts you because
he killed himself. —What kind of sign is this?
What could it mean? I leave my wedding ring
on the dresser top. Wear comfortable shoes.
Drive to City of Hope, in the desert,
where in the nineteen twenties and thirties
tuberculosis patients came to die.

Some survived, of course. Like Eugene O'Neill,
though he didn't convalesce here. He's been
a hero of mine—till lately. *Long Day's
Journey into Night* felt like a memoir
of my own childhood. Just better written,
more whiskey. Morphine. I saw it in school
and walked out of there like I was walking
on air. I worshipped him. But I fear him
now, his life's tragedy. I want to live
comedies now. I disrobe. Nurses plug
a hose blowing warm air into a hole
in my paper gown. Put pink socks on me.
Make a pin cushion of me. Dr. Fong,
my surgeon, is world famous. He's smiling
as I roll into the operating
theater. Just another workday for them.
Blue gowns and masks. The bold white freezing room.
More intros offered. Ceiling lights spinning
like UFOs. Or medical halos.

FONG: Oh, about six hours. We'll open you up
along the same incision the other
surgeon used for your colon resection
in the spring. We'll pull your stomach muscles
out of the way, which may be difficult
because you're surprisingly muscly!
ha ha ha. We have to reach that corner
of your liver next to your diaphragm
here, on this side. Feel it? We're going to take
about fifteen percent of your liver,
at least that's the plan. Your gallbladder too,
just for good measure. Ha ha ha. It's good
you'll be wide open! We'll see more that way,
lesions the scans have missed. I'll feel around.
—Don't worry! I've done this a thousand times.
What does Malcolm Gladwell say? Anyway,
I've got that beat. I've got a good feeling
about you. Feeling sleepy? Breathe in, Dan.
Breathe in. You like Trump? How are we feeling
about Syria?

DAN: Did he ask me that?   *Lights slowly*

FONG: Oceans of refugees, children drowning *dimming.*
off Greece.

DAN: A while back I gave him my play
about you, Paul. Inscribed. I was hoping
he might surgeon a little bit harder

if he liked my playwriting. He'd studied
medieval lit at Brown. The next visit
he said he'd tried to read my play. Teared up
as he confessed. It was too sad! he cried
—I couldn't finish! He seems confused, Paul,
as people sometimes are, as to whether
you're a real person or just somebody
I made up. They think I'm you. I confuse
myself sometimes too.

FONG: —We have to take care
of this man!   *Lights*

DAN: The surgeon is instructing   *rising.*
the nurses as I surface. With my wife
beside me. The bleeping. Numb dizziness.
This new incision runs from just below
my navel to my breasts. Some kind of glue,   *The sound*
smoky like a skid mark on the highway,   *of the sea, almost*
holds my belly together. My spare tire,   *imperceptible.*
such as it is, is lumpy, and I think
the least they could have done is given me
some lipo while they were in there. Each breath's
a knife in my side. Hiccupping acid's
burning my throat.

FONG: This bearded young man is
a war reporter! We need him healthy
so he can continue to run away
from the Taliban—!

DAN: Though I've been nowhere
besides Europe. The Arctic once with you,
of course. A few other places.

NURSE: Wake up,   *Late night.*

DAN: whispers the nurse.

NURSE: Your heart rate is
too high. Breathe into this tube. We need you
breathing. —We don't want you developing
pneumonia.

DAN: —I have pneumonia?

NURSE: Not yet.

DAN: Where's my wife? Where's—Jessica? —Who are you?

EUGENE: Eugene.

DAN: Like O'Neill?

EDMUND: Call me Edmund.

DAN: Why—?

EDMUND: Everything comes from and must return to
the sea. Aboard the HMS *Terror*   *Now louder,*

bound for the pole. In search of safe passage   *the sound of*
out of Syria. Blood moon in the trades.   *the sea.*
Flying spume, a cargo of bawling babes
below, towering masts with shroud-like sails
whipping in the wind. —Imagine curtains
drawn back by an unseen hand: an instant
to see. —Do you see? Until the curtains
close again, and we find ourselves alone
with the ice closing in. We drop anchor
for winter. How will we survive? —Our grins
grow scurvy. We should not have been born men,
Dan. We should have been born albatrosses
or politicians. We will always be
strangers in this world, you and I, always
a little too much in love with—

DAN: No! —No!
—Get away from me!

NURSE: —Mr. O'Brien?
We've got a shot of Ativan for you.
Breathe in. Breathe in. Breathe in. That's better. Sleep
if you can.

DAN: The next morning: *Morning.*
FONG: Stand and walk,
DAN: says Dr. Fong. He commands me. Jesus
couldn't have said it better.

FONG: You'll have to
make him,
DAN: he tells my wife.
FONG: When I donate
my time, operating on servicemen
and -women with shrapnel in their organs
from the roadside bombs—their comrades-in-arms
sit bedside, in this chair. And every hour
they stand their soldier up, they take his arm
and they lead him from bed to chair, from chair
to window, from window into the hall
and within four, five days they're home. So lead
your soldier, Mrs. O'Brien. You too
will be home soon, I promise. And this scar
will vanish, mostly. Trust me. I began
in cosmetic surgery. I know how
to hide my scars.

DAN: The Dilaudid pump dulls
the pain. The room's a sea-slick deck. My mouth
is parched, limbs shaking. Standing. My wife grasps

my feeble hand. From bed to chair, from chair
to window. As the days pass. A heat wave
shimmers the mountains, the flashing shoreline
of distant cars. We walk from the window
into the hall where I glance through doorways   *Fluorescent light.*
at all the unfortunates, some who'll live,
many who won't. Two women in hijabs   *Nighttime.*
huddle around a phone with their doctor
involving an interpreter elsewhere
to explain the graft-versus-host disease
that's killing their father. I look away,
stop listening.

JESSICA: I've been offered a gig
hosting a game show,

DAN: Jessica mentions
as we shuffle along.

JESSICA: It's a big hit
in like England. I don't really like it—
kids saying the darnedest things, stuff like that—
but the pay's ridiculous. We wouldn't
have to worry about these bills, about
college for Bebe. About anything
for Bebe, really. What do you think, Dan,
should we do it?

DAN: The morning we're leaving   *The sense of light*
the hospital, I find myself praying   *at the end*
for an angel. Even though I suspect   *of a tunnel*
if angels exist they're busy somewhere
like Syria.

WOMAN: —I need to talk to *him*,   *growing until*
DAN: says an ancient woman at reception   *the end of*
as I'm slumped in my wheelchair. She's arrayed   *this scene.*
all in purple, even a purple hat,
purple shoes, like some magical grandma
in an Oscar-winning film. Hobbling
toward me—hands outstretched:

WOMAN: I need to talk
to this young man. —You're going to have long days,
DAN: she says, squeezing my hands,
WOMAN: long days, long days
on this earth. Keep trusting.

DAN: —Then walks outside
wishing everybody here a happy
holiday.

7: SUSHI

PAUL: I had this nightmare last night. There I was
                   rising up through an underground garage
                   until the elevator opened on
                   Perfumes. A floor of trial makeovers
                   for aging starlets. Puffed-up lizard lips,
                   bugged-out eyelids. I couldn't stop screaming
                   in the dream. —So what are we feeling like?   *Restaurant,*
                   You guys decide.   *early evening.*

DAN: You want us to order
                   for you?

PAUL: I don't know what any of this
                   gobbledygook means.

JESSICA: You want sushi though,
                   right?

PAUL: asks Jessica.

JESSICA: This was your idea.

PAUL: That's right.

JESSICA: Because Dan can't have the sushi
                   because of chemo. His blood counts.

PAUL: That's right.

JESSICA: Have you ever even had sushi, Paul?
                   It's raw.

PAUL: Are you allowed to eat raw fish,
                   Jessica?

DAN: She's a year out from treatment
                   with no evidence of disease.

PAUL: That's right.
                   That's good.

DAN: That's great.

PAUL: —Are you hearing something?

DAN: Like what?

PAUL: —Like a—whirring or—some machine?

DAN: That's just my pump.

PAUL: What?

DAN: The needle's hidden
                   underneath my sleeve. See? The tube snakes down
                   inside my shirt, and the pump's tucked inside
                   my fanny pack here—

PAUL: I was wondering
                   about all that.

DAN: And intermittently
                   it fires another round of fluorouacil
                   into my veins.

PAUL: Are you going to wear that
                      in our meetings?
DAN: Well you only hear it
                      during the awkward pauses. —There it goes
                      again.
PAUL: Ha ha ha.
JESSICA: He has to wear it,
PAUL: says Jessica.
DAN: For a few days,
PAUL: says Dan.
DAN: And I'm going to have to wear a face mask
                      at the meetings too.
PAUL: What like a hockey—?
DAN: Like—surgical mask—you know, for like germs.
PAUL: You're right, you can really hear that machine
                      during the awkward pauses.
DAN: —Ha ha ha!
PAUL: God, you guys really have had an annus
                      horribilis, haven't you?
JESSICA: Is that how
                      you say it?
PAUL: What did you think it was, Jess—?
JESSICA: Anus?
PAUL: Ha ha ha you've had a rectum
                      horribilis!
DAN: Well a sigmoid colon
                      horribilis to be accurate—
PAUL: Hey!
                      You're a semicolon now, Dan!
DAN: Good one.
PAUL: Ha ha ha! —Talk about lightning striking
                      twice. Christ. Did you two piss somebody off
                      in a previous life? Maybe Putin
                      poisoned you.
DAN: We threw a dinner party
                      once. This woman was a psychiatrist,
                      and she sat on our couch with her bare feet
                      tucked up beneath her like she was thirteen
                      and her husband, a screenwriter, asked us
                      which idea we found most frightening: the death
                      of our spouse, or our own death. The answer
                      would be revealing, he promised. We live
                      with the possibility that our child
                      could grow up without either one of us.
                      They're divorced now, by the way. Last I heard.

PAUL: But what was your answer? —To the question
he was asking about fear—

DAN: Oh, we changed
the subject. I think I'm going to order
the tofu teriyaki.

PAUL: That sounds safe,
I'll do that too. —Hey is that the actor
from *Entourage*?

DAN: From where?

PAUL: You know that guy
who used to be bald on *Seinfeld* before
he got like those hair plugs or weaves and then
sushi poisoning?

DAN: All of this happened
in real life?

PAUL: No, it's just some normal guy.

DAN: There's a lot of us.

PAUL: So I've been thinking:
why don't I just stick around till Monday
for like a postmortem? I mean we'll sell
this pitch, or we won't. And if nothing else
we can go to Disneyland.

JESSICA: I don't know,

PAUL: says Jessica.

JESSICA: Dan's got a phobia
of amusement parks. Adults in costumes
freak him out.

PAUL: How so, Dan?

DAN: It feels tragic.

PAUL: —Well then you picked the wrong profession, man!
—The theatre? —With costumes?

JESSICA: Are you okay
on an air bed, Paul? Because you're welcome
to the couch.

PAUL: Thanks, Jess, I prefer the floor
actually. Also I want to get down
on the same level as your little girl.
You know: roughhouse. What's her name?

JESSICA: Isobel
but we call her Bebe—

PAUL: And your schnauzer,
what's his name?

JESSICA: Emma.

PAUL: Even though I tend
to despise dogs. Because I think of them

as agents of cosmic retribution,
ha ha ha. Also I'd like to learn how
to windsurf, if there's time. Are my eyebrows
too bushy? I forgot to trim before
leaving home. Maybe you could shave your neck,
Dan. —You look like a Sasquatch!

JESSICA: Are you tense
about these meetings, Paul? I've pitched a lot
and it's real.

PAUL: Yes and no, Jess. I'm used to
my intestines churning from the terror
of, you know, gunfire. Now I'm terrified
of coming home to the same life.

JESSICA: That's hard.
PAUL: I've been reading some books: *Difficult Men:*
Behind the Scenes of a Revolution
in TV.

JESSICA: That sounds helpful. Right, Dan? —Dan?
PAUL: The cover says something like From Tony
Soprano to Walter White: Psychopaths
Who Speak to Our Psychotic Times. It's fun
to envision our future creations
killing each other. Themselves. I'm convinced
we're the legitimate heirs to the throne
of critically adored and sadistic
TV for grownups. Grandiosity's
my métier, and you can normalize
our dialogue, right Dan?

DAN: Let's order now,
don't you think?

JESSICA: I think you should consider,   *Late evening.*
DAN: says Jessica, as we fall into bed,
JESSICA: throwing this pitch.
DAN: Throwing? like a boxer?
JESSICA: All I mean is maybe it's a good thing
nobody's going to buy it.

DAN: Nobody's—?
JESSICA: Well they're not, Dan. You're aware of that, right?
—It would be a major coup, let's put it
that way.

DAN: But you've been encouraging me
for months now—

JESSICA: I just wanted you to have
something. You know.

DAN: You've been humoring me?

JESSICA: I mean—what do *I* know? I don't know how
to sell a show.

DAN: Yes, you actually do.

JESSICA: But this is a drama. About war.

DAN: So?

JESSICA: So it's going to be a challenge.

DAN: We need
the money.

JESSICA: We always need the money.

DAN: Thanks for your support.

JESSICA: And neither of you
has any kind of track record in—

DAN: Hey,
I'm an award-winning poet-playwright!

JESSICA: Oh, Dan.

DAN: Oh what?

JESSICA: Let's just say I'm relieved.
Because I don't think you could stand writing
with Paul anyway.

DAN: Please, lower your voice—

JESSICA: He's downstairs!

DAN: —He could be standing outside
our door here!

JESSICA: You're kind of proving my point!
He's intense. He's intense. Maybe it's best
if you move on.

DAN: From writing about Paul?

JESSICA: Maybe. No more war. —Why do you want to
write this as a TV show anyway?
That's not you.

DAN: I don't know. Maybe it is
me now.

JESSICA: I hear that.

DAN: Maybe I'm done with
writing alone. Maybe I want a house
with some grass outside. Maybe I deserve
a paycheck.

JESSICA: Why don't we write something then
together?

DAN: You and me?

JESSICA: Is that crazy?

DAN: Like a comedy?

JESSICA: It would have to be
funny if I'm involved.

DAN: —I just don't know

if I'm ready to give up yet.

JESSICA: Give up
on Paul?

DAN: I just keep having this feeling,
if I can sell this show, with Paul, somehow
—I'll win.

JESSICA: Are you crying?

DAN: It's the chemo.

JESSICA: You're going to survive.

DAN: You're going to survive
too.

JESSICA: I know.

DAN: I know too. I keep thinking
about this poem.

JESSICA: Of yours?

DAN: Seamus Heaney.

JESSICA: Oh him.

DAN: About Diarmuid and Grainne.

JESSICA: Who?

DAN: Just an Irish myth. But anyway,
in this poem Heaney says he and his wife
are lying on a hillside in Ireland
in their sleeping bags, their faces exposed
to the elements. Like stone effigies,
is how describes it. And he recalls
the night they first kissed. A hotel somewhere.
Her deliberate kiss, is how he puts it,
to raise us toward the lovely, painful
covenants of flesh. I'm paraphrasing
but you get the picture.

JESSICA: That's beautiful.

DAN: Can I kiss you?

JESSICA: We don't kiss anymore.

DAN: I'm too scared.

JESSICA: So am I.

DAN: Why don't we try
a deliberate kiss then?

JESSICA: All right.

DAN: All right.

PAUL: Sorry to interrupt—   *Morning.*

DAN: The next morning
we're rehearsing our pitch.

PAUL: But it feels like
we're starting to depress them.

DAN: Depress whom?

PAUL: The Executives. This is Hollywood.

DAN: So?

PAUL: So they're expecting the Combat Sex
and the Bang Bang!

DAN: So then what would you change?

PAUL: Your performance, for one.

DAN: My—?

PAUL: Imagine
you're an actor onstage and the natives
are starting to get restless—

DAN: Listen Paul,
I know how to handle my audience—

PAUL: —Like somebody should kill somebody—

DAN: Hey!
I'm not going to, you know, tap dance for them
or like—wear a lot of hats—!

PAUL: Okay, Dan,
but still you've got to *surprise* us! —Them!

DAN: Paul,
let's just get through this run-through like one time,
okay?

PAUL: —Because I'm a good example
of somebody who can't pay attention
very well.

DAN: Ha ha ha!

PAUL: Ha ha ha!

DAN: Paul,
I feel your comments about our pitch—

PAUL: Yes.

DAN: Have become sort of—

PAUL: What.

DAN: Fear-based.

PAUL: —They *are*
fear-based! —My whole life is fear-based!

DAN: —So's mine!
—With the cancer! —And my approach to fear
is to squelch it. Squeeze it. Strangle the life
out of my fear.

PAUL: Okay. Just don't be shocked
when they get bored.

DAN: —If they're bored it's because
we can't get through like two minutes of this
fucking pitch without you stopping to give
me your fucking notes!

PAUL: Look, I may be wrong

                            and if I am: my bad. Which reminds me,
                            we need to inject more gallows humor
                            into this thing.

DAN: Why don't we take a break
                            and make some more coffee.

PAUL: —Oh, and cut down
                            your intro, Dan.

DAN: I'm just being myself.

PAUL: Okay, but telling them you first heard me
                            on *NPR*—?

DAN: So?

PAUL: Why don't you tell them
                            you had like a shotgun in your mouth and
                            hearing my voice on *Fresh Air* made you weep
                            and put the gun down—

DAN: I don't even own
                            a gun—!

PAUL: Then why did you first write to me?
                            —Do you know?

DAN: I know.

PAUL: Then tell me! —Tell them!

DAN: I thought I was you. I identified
                            with you—too closely. With the loneliness.
                            Guilt. About my family. Leaving them all
                            behind—though truly they left me. You know
                            the story. I was suffering. Like you
                            I felt cursed—

PAUL: Why don't you say some of that
                            in the intro?

DAN: Whatever.

PAUL: The point is
                            you've got to find a way to *move* them, Dan.

DAN: —And you've got to move them too, Paul!

PAUL: Okay.

DAN: And not go off on these tangents.

PAUL: Okay.

DAN: And you've got to keep track of time because
                            you don't have a very good sense of time!

PAUL: I get that a lot.

DAN: And stop rattling on
                            in this manic rapid-fire—

PAUL: Wait I talk
                            manically?

DAN: —You see this is exactly
                            what I didn't want to do!

PAUL: This is how
I talk, Dan! —Why didn't you tell me this
earlier when I could've done something
about it?

DAN: Because I didn't want to
start a fight!

PAUL: But if you tell me today
I won't be manic tomorrow!

DAN: I *am*
telling you now!

PAUL: Okay but I wasn't
getting it, Dan!

DAN: Okay.

PAUL: —I'm used to blunt
coworkers!

DAN: I was exaggerating
because you pushed me.

PAUL: I want to be sliced
and diced here. You don't know how important
this pitch is to me. I've looked at houses,
sail boats. I've told everybody I know:
That's it, I'm done. You've got your wife's career
to fall back on.

DAN: In what way?

PAUL: That game show
you told me about—

DAN: She's not hosting that
anymore.

PAUL: What happened?

DAN: What's important
is we relax.

PAUL: Okay.

DAN: And not be scared
of scaring them.

PAUL: Okay.

DAN: Compensating
with things like Combat Sex and the Bang Bang—

PAUL: I know! —I've been obsessed!

DAN: And this is why
you shouldn't be reading these how-to books
about Hollywood—

PAUL: You're right, you're right, Dan,
I've been in my head.

DAN: You're scared.

PAUL: I should not

be reading that junk—it's *junk!*

DAN: It's okay
you're scared. I am too.

PAUL: I've been searching for
an answer.

DAN: And all we can do is ask:
We have this story and do you want to
help us tell it?

PAUL: Help us sell it.

DAN: That too.

PAUL: Okay, Dan.

DAN: Okay, Paul.

PAUL: I'm real sorry
we fought.

DAN: Me too.

PAUL: This is like the worst fight
I've had in my life.

DAN: It wasn't that bad.

PAUL: Do you think we can still be friends?

DAN: Listen,
Paul. Let's just pitch this thing. Okay?

PAUL: Okay,
Dan. And if I sound manic please punch me
in the face.

EXEC: —Apologies, gentlemen,   *New morning.*

PAUL: says the Exec,

EXEC: but my twins pitched a fit
on the PCH en route to preschool
in Malibu.

PAUL: Ha ha ha—must be nice!

EXEC: And then I got stuck in this breakfast thing
with Name Redacted—

PAUL: Oh I love that show!

EXEC: —where we were just waiting for X to show,
but his father's been on the downward slope
like *forever*. And I'm like, X—come on!
And he's like, What? my father's retreated
to San Carlos. And I'm all, Where the hell
is San Carlos? And he goes, On the Sea
of Cortez. So I ask, Where is the Sea
of Cortez?—even though I don't care if
it's the Sea of Fucking Galilee, when
Name Redacted's in town the Show Runner
comes to breakfast! —Brunch, at least.

PAUL: —Ha ha ha!

EXEC:	What's with the mask?
PAUL:	It's nothing, it's cancer.
DAN:	My immune system—
PAUL:	Ignore it. I do.
DAN:	The Executive looks like a Nordic
	dominatrix. Her two assistants like
	bearded mute masochists. Horned-rim glasses
	in impassive faces.
PAUL:	I've got pictures

A few of these

	here on my phone. I was travelling alone

vivid photos.

	with the al-Nusra rebels, the city
	like a lunar landscape, with Scud missiles
	pulverizing apartment blocks. Digging
	children out, mostly dead—
EXEC:	I can't even
	begin to imagine—!
PAUL:	Well that went well.
DAN:	You think?
PAUL:	She seemed disturbed.
DAN:	Is that the goal?
EXEC:	Sorry to keep you waiting.

New morning.

DAN:	This exec
	is blonde too. Sour-faced,
PAUL:	she seems already
	disappointed.
DAN:	A whiskey-voiced, whiskered
	hipster rides a scooter.
PAUL:	Dan says:
DAN:	This mask
	is just a precaution.
EXEC:	It's disturbing,
DAN:	smiles the Blonde Exec,
EXEC:	just seeing your eyes.
EXEC 2:	Shit guys we forgot to give our orders
	for lunch—wait two secs.
PAUL:	—It's gallows humor,
DAN:	explains the War Reporter.
PAUL:	If you like
	your jokes-on-a-rope then you'll love the world
	of _The Zone._
EXEC 2:	Wait—is that your title, bro?
EXEC:	_The Zone_'s a diet. I've tried it.
EXEC 2:	Sounds like
	a downer, dude.
PAUL:	—It's the new Rwanda!

DAN: Paul's being funny.
EXEC: We're running over
                I'm sad to say—
EXEC 2:   We've got a lunch meeting
                in like three.
PAUL: Why don't we all continue
                this convo at the Cheesecake Factory
                next door?
EXEC 2:   Thanks for dropping by.
EXEC: Wow. Just—wow.
DAN: Well that went well.
PAUL: We have glimpsed the future
                and they are young,
DAN: murmurs Paul. But one day
                they'll suffer too,
PAUL: soothes the Poet. —You tired,
                Dan? You sure? What I can see of your face
                looks pale. —Let's take a breather.
EXEC: —What is this,   *New morning.*
                a doctor-drama?
PAUL: glad-hands another
                bearded young Turk, horn-rimmed glasses.
DAN: Congrats
                on the Emmy,
PAUL: Dan says. So savvy.
EXEC: Thanks,
                but when you hop in bed with a name like
                Name Redacted—! We're all feeling pretty
                well jazzed today. The question is can we
                do it again? Which is where you two jerks
                come in! Ha ha ha.   *Pic of*
PAUL: I've always been one   *Aleppo*
                for lost causes—   *in ruins.*
EXEC: So maybe I'm jumping
                the gun here, guys. Because your world is good
                in terms of its scope, I'm feeling the soap
                opera aspect here—but what's the story
                of your Season One in just one word?
PAUL: Fish
                -out-of-water.
DAN: Truth-teller-in-exile,
PAUL: says Dan. We're using hyphens.
EXEC: —What a treat
                to have met you.
PAUL: That could have gone much worse,

considering he's a man.

DAN: A voice speaks   *New morning.*
via speakerphone.

EXEC: Bry's at Comic-Con
in San Diego. —Say hi, Bry.

BRY: —Hello,
Carrie! —Greetings, guys!

CARRIE: Are you cosplaying
as something in particular?

DAN: Carrie
winks at us like a seizure.

PAUL: There's a man   *Helicopters*
in the corner, beardless, crew cut.   *far off.*

BRY: Pardon?

PAUL: answers the Voice of Bry.

DAN: Why don't you start
this time, Paul.

PAUL: Okay. As we all know war
holds eternal appeal. Homer knew that,
Shakespeare. Tom Hanks. That Somali street kid *Helicopters*
sporting our corpse's goggles while flashing *closer.*
my camera the finger. Burnt flesh on sticks.
Teeth in handkerchiefs. Speaking to the dead
soldier, I said—sorry, I get choked up   *The sound*
just talking about this—still. His children *of the mob.*
have children now.

DAN: Take a tissue, Paul. Here,
drink some water.

CARRIE: Okay, any questions,
Bryan? —Bry-Bry, you still there?

BRY-BRY: So sorry,
must've muted my end. —Outstanding job,
everybody!

PAUL: Can everybody see
that guy in the corner? With the smooth face *The ghost*
and the crew cut? Is he wearing khakis? *of Paul's Pulitzer*
are his legs broken? Are those bullet holes *photograph.*
in his body? He looks like a soldier
I know.

EXEC 3:   If you sell this I will own it
forever.

PAUL: —Ha ha ha!

DAN: Nobody else
is here, Paul. Just us.

PAUL: Carrie cried! Real tears

welled up in her blue eyes!

DAN: While reception
validates our parking.

PAUL: Going down, down,
down—

DAN: Paul's mimicking the elevator's
electronic drone. —You know my head-shrink
works in this building, Paul.

PAUL: That's right.

DAN: High noon   *High noon.*
in a space-age solarium, white light
of the west side,

PAUL: two plumpish guys wearing
beards and glasses,

DAN: like Stanley Kubrick clones.

EXEC 1:   Do any of our protagonists like
get kidnapped?

DAN: asks Kubrick Number One.

PAUL: —Sure!

EXEC 2:   Beaten?

PAUL: asks Number Two.

EXEC 2:   Tortured?

PAUL: —Why not?

DAN: You want that, right?

PAUL: You know I'm reminded   *A cloud*
of this one time a rebel was cutting   *obscures*
open the body of a loyalist   *the sun.*
in a crater. Hacking like a husband
at a barbecue. Gouging a fish mouth
into the lifeless breast, through which he plucks
a heart and lays it on a plank across
the corpse's solar plexus. —You're carving
him a valentine! cries the cameraman
off screen. Embarrassed birdsong, light shredding
of human meat. Gristle-flicking. He lifts
the heart with knife in hand. The other hand
scoops up a hunk of lung. We will devour
your hearts and livers, you mercenaries
of Bashar the Pig! Then ritually bites
into flesh that breathed. Not heart, or liver
as was reported. Allahu akbar!
voices had been shouting. God is greater   *By now the light*
than whom? This cannibal is just a man   *is strange,*
from Homs, who before the spring sold lamb's meat
in the streets. Teased olive branches beneath

the noses of Bashar's dogs. A woman   *another time*
and child chanting—two shots, his brother stooped   *and place.*
to help—through the neck, he bled out next. More
friends and a lover lost. Police called him
on his cellphone so he could feel the sound
of his parents beaten. And remember
that dead loyalist had a video
in his phone: girls made to watch their mother
raped with sticks. When their turns came. Then all stabbed
as if clinically. You weren't bothered
by any of that—why? Picture yourself
in my shoes, he said. Like I told the ghost
of that American soldier years ago
in Mogadishu: *I didn't want to*
do this, I had to do this. It is true
I have changed. I have become the Angel
of Death. Here to devour the hearts of men
like beasts.   *The white light*

EXEC 2:   That's wild.   *of the west side*
EXEC 1:   That's good TV right there.   *returns.*
EXEC 2:   We can market that.
EXEC 1:   And is the idea
            you two would write this pilot together?
DAN: If you pay us enough.
PAUL: —Please!
EXEC 2:   How's your health,
            Paul, your—mental—?
PAUL: Ha ha ha, I'm feeling
            much better, thanks!
DAN: He's fine—
EXEC 1:   Is *your* health, Dan,
            going to be an obstacle?
DAN: Time will tell,
            or at least that's what my doctors have been
            telling me.
PAUL: —Ha ha ha!
EXEC 2:   Interesting stuff.
            We'll be in touch.
PAUL: I'm worried I'm having
            an actual breakdown,
DAN: says Paul. I feel
            like throwing up.
PAUL: My gums ache. Head's pounding
            like I have a fever.
DAN: While we're waiting

```
                    at the valet stand in the sun.
PAUL:                                —You think
                    they're going to buy it?
DAN:                                 I don't know—
PAUL:                                           They said
                    interesting.
DAN:                        That could go either way though.
PAUL:               They'll be in touch.
DAN:                              They will.
PAUL:                                    They get to ask,
                    Who lives and dies? But then they slink away
                    to their screening rooms. To be really real,
                    you know, the characters who have to die
                    are the ones we love the most.
DAN:                                       So—sushi?
PAUL:               Ha ha ha. Here's our car.
DAN:                                 A conference call
                    weeks later, with Paul home in Vancouver,
                    me at my desk and Ari our fixer
                    in Studio City—
ARI:                            So the news is
                    everybody passed. Yeah. Nobody cares
                    about war anymore. Nobody likes
                    journalists much these days either. Also
                    they couldn't tell the good guys from the bad,
                    somebody mentioned. Re: your pitch. And while
                    your story's just tragic, guys, just tragic,
                    the truth is it would cost too much to shoot.
                    But let's touch base down the line and maybe
                    have Alice try and set up another
                    brunch?
```

8: RAISING THE TERROR

```
DAN:                Dear Paul. This last stretch of chemo is like
                    what I imagine it might be like to
                    get kidnapped. Be held hostage. Like we'd planned
                    to kidnap our young cub reporter Dan,
                    in our show, if ever we'd been given
                    the green light. I'm bedbound. Leukocytes low
                    again. Can't run. Walking up and down stairs
                    sends my heart racing. It's cumulative,
                    they keep telling me. Some don't make it. Some
```

are killed by the cure. Our next-door neighbor
who many months ago when she was told
about my cancer in our driveway joked,
Stay away from me!—was just diagnosed
with ovarian. We share a wall. Well,
she smiled, you've got to pay to skate. I cry
a lot. Then cry some more. I'm letting go
of something. Something I need to let go
but it hurts. Merry Christmas to you, Paul,
and Happy New Year. After a few days
I'll feel much better. A few months more and
I'll be through.

PAUL: Decca texted directions
to this book launch in Tribeca. She works
for the publisher who just bought my pitch
for a work of narrative nonfiction
about the discovery of that lost
Franklin expedition. But all I found
were millennials, bearded, glasses, high
on the stoop. Where's the party? They pointed
upstairs. Into this purely white hallway
with numberless doors. Cocking my ears for
the murmur of revelry. In a loft
stuffed with Coptic papyrus and tribal   *The murmur*
statues of phalluses. Something playing   *of revelry and*
like ABBA on ludes. Everybody looked   *music.*
self-important. Like assholes. I'd rather
be watching *Game of Thrones* at the hotel
Decca paid for. So I give this soirée
one last look-see, and slipping out the door
things only become more mysterious
as I wander, snow falling like cinders
from Freedom Tower. Not even the wind
to sing for the dead I've known. I miss you
now more than ever, my friend. Write to me
when you can.

DAN: My scar is healing. Thinning.
Like a vanishing pink crack in the vase
of my pale skin. My hair is growing back
straight and black. Jessica says I'm aging
backward. I don't trust her. But recent scans
have been clear. My blood work's good. They tell me
there's no evidence of disease. For now
and who knows how long. There's a decent chance
I'm already cured, one doctor mentioned

casually. I'll take it. I go running
on the beach again. Slowly, and slowly
running faster. My hands and feet are numb
still, the neuropathy. They may remain
that way, I've been told. Some things will return
and some won't. Time will tell. Like, is the war
over? Or is this just an armistice?
Congratulations on your retirement
from journalism, by the way. You've done
the right thing, Paul. —And congratulations
also on that book deal! I feel jealous
because I wanted to be there with you
when you discovered the *Terror*. I know
it wasn't the *Terror* but *Erebus*
you found first. And of course I'm well aware
you weren't really the discoverer,
but you were there. And you wrote about it.
And I'm proud of you. I can't wait to read
your book.

PAUL: A chopper pilot patrolling
the stone shore of Queen Maud Gulf—when he spies
a twinkling bit of iron, rusted, shaped
like a tuning fork, stamped with the logo
of the Royal Navy.

DAN: I'm forgetting
this year already. But some memories
resurface. I'm feeling optimistic
when I'm not terrified. I'm forgetting
your voice, Paul. It's getting harder to hear
your voice. Harder to write you.

PAUL: We deploy
our arsenal, robot subs and multi
-beam 3D sonar towfishes, sidescan
relics as backups, a silver bullet
-nosed beauty with black fins that delivers
that Eureka! moment—when the Falcon
turns its dread eye on the wreck.

DAN: Imagine
resurrecting the ship. With Lord Franklin
bald and stout in his mutton chops. Frozen
impeccably below. His skin like bronze
statuary. Eyes like split marble, teeth
like gruesome walrus tusks on account of
the scurvy smile. Imagine his sailors,

those who died trying to escape across
the ice, those butchered and cooked in their own
tin kettles: they dig themselves out of cairns,
they stand themselves up on the permafrost.
With bodies whole and young again, they heave
upon the drag ropes until the *Terror*
rises out of the water and onto
dry land. Or the ice anyway, sparkling
in the sun. Time will tell. Has told. We must
give thanks. We must wait and see. Safe travels,
my friend.

9: RESTORING THE ROOM

	A theater's
	rehearsal room.

So that's it. I mean, that's what I've written
so far. How much time do we have left for
discussion?

DIRECTOR: We have to vacate like—now,

DAN: says Neel the Director.

DRAMATURG: Another group's
reserved the room,

DAN: says Joy the Dramaturg.

ACTOR 1:   —I've got a table-read in like an hour,

DAN: says the actor who played me.

ACTOR 1:   At Sony.

DAN: The older actor who played Paul—

ACTOR 2:   guffaws.

DAN: I'm going to take notes, okay guys? I hope
you don't mind. I'm thinking this could become
the end of our play? like an epilogue
of some kind. And really, I can't thank you
enough. I haven't even heard the play
until right now—

NEEL: Let's talk and tidy up
at the same time,

DAN: says Neel the Director.

JOY: And we're so glad,

DAN: says Joy the Dramaturg,

JOY: Paul could join us.

DAN: —Well thanks for flying him
all the way here, the hotel. I'm afraid
to hear his thoughts. You know he never saw

that other play I wrote about him?

NEEL: —What?

DAN: exclaims Neel the Director. —I don't mind.
           I've been relieved. It took the pressure off.
           But it does makes me wonder: Why this one,
           Paul? What are you thinking?

PAUL: This has been like
           the coolest group therapy.

EVERYBODY: Ha ha ha!

PAUL: Because you brought back the good memories
           with the bad. But really it's been a hoot
           just to be able to sit here and watch
           art get made. I should have been a writer
           like you, Dan.

DAN: Maybe I should've been one
           like you.

PAUL: —Oh God I hope not!

DAN: —And I hope
           you're okay with the poetic license
           I've taken.

JOY: Like?

DAN: asks Joy the Dramaturg.

PAUL: Well, like our TV pitch didn't happen
           this year—

DAN: It happened a long time ago.

NEEL: —What?

DAN: exclaims Neel the Director.

PAUL: That's right,

DAN: says Paul.

PAUL: You won't find any journalists
           in Syria now. That is, American
           journalists.

JOY: Because I was going to say,

PAUL: says Joy,

JOY: isn't ISIS pretty much dead?
           And the migrant crisis is winding down—

PAUL: Is it?

JOY: Well we're not hearing about it
           anymore.

PAUL: That's right.

DAN: Neel's still shocked. He says:

NEEL: —But your cancer's real.

DAN: Oh yeah, that happened
           recently. While I wrote this. It was good

having something like this to distract me,
ha ha ha.

PAUL: And Syria's real,

DAN: says Paul.

PAUL: Real as cancer.

DAN: I exaggerated
all the scenes with the wives too, like Zelda,
how she's skeptical of our TV pitch—

PAUL: She's skeptical of all this shit!

DAN: —This play
included?

JOY: I think it's fascinating,

DAN: says Joy the Dramaturg,

JOY: how you've crafted
a play instead of a TV show.

DAN: Why?

JOY: Plays can be honest. Tell the truth.

DAN: Can they?

JOY: There's less money at stake.

DAN: Well *that* is true.

NEEL: —So is this all a dream?

DAN: the director
Neel wonders.

NEEL   Maybe it's all the sickness
and death in the play—

DAN: And the opiates—

NEEL: And I know something about this because
I was almost killed by West Nile Virus
several years ago. You may have noticed
I walk with a slight limp. I basically
had polio. And you've captured that, Dan,
in this play, for better or worse, that sense
of living in limbo. Living between
life and death. Whether we're in Syria
or Santa Monica, or Vancouver
or Hollywood. —Wow, thanks everybody
for a fascinating day! And to Dan
—happy rewriting!

DAN: —Bye!

JOY: How's your health now?

DAN: asks Joy. Well my blood tests look good. Clear scans
still. I've got another scan on Wednesday
so touch wood. Thank you.

ACTOR 1:   —Oh and you used spume

                                              twice,
DAN: yawns the younger actor.
ACTOR 1:   In the play.
                          Before I forget. Can you use spume twice?
DAN: The older actor cracks:
ACTOR 2:   Can you use spume
                          once?
DAN: Are you guys speaking as actors now
                          or freelance dramaturgs?
PAUL: —Are we allowed
                          to give feedback?
DAN: asks Paul.
PAUL: Like, opinions?
DAN: That's what you're here for—
PAUL: I just wouldn't say
                          filleted. It's the only thing I thought
                          sounded false.
DAN: Consider it deleted.
                          That's it?
PAUL: Your play seems pretty done to me:
                          two friends confronting death in their own way,
                          desperate to make a new life in the world
                          of TV. It's hilarious.
DAN: It's sad
                          too. Bittersweet, maybe. A chronicle
                          of change, moving on. You've got your new book
                          about Franklin. I'm selling this sitcom
                          with my wife.
PAUL: —I feel like you're breaking up
                          with me!
DAN: —It's not you it's me!
PAUL: Ha ha ha!
DAN: Ha ha ha!
JOY: And what about *your* health, Paul?
DAN: asks Joy.
JOY: Your mental health. Are you happy
                          now that you're no longer a journalist?
DAN: That's something I've wanted to ask you too,
                          Paul: Do you still feel haunted by the ghost
                          of Staff-Sergeant William David Cleveland
                          in Mogadishu? Among other ghosts.
                          —Can a haunting ever end?
PAUL: You'll stop me
                          if this gets boring, I mean it mainly
                          for entertainment value. But after

	one of the performances of your play,
	Dan—like Dan said, I never saw the play
	but I'd go do like these flashbacks they're called—?
DAN:	Talkbacks.
PAUL:	And this one time this lady asked:
	How do you know the ghost of that soldier
	in Mogadishu meant to threaten you?
	If you do this, he said, I will own you
	forever. What else could he have meant? Well
	maybe he meant you'll never be the same
	again. Good and bad. You've changed.
DAN:	—Actually,
	Paul, I suggested that to you.
PAUL:	—*You* did?
DAN:	I wrote it into our previous play.
	I'll probably write it into this play too.
PAUL:	—You see? This is what I'm talking about!
	Why don't you write a play about this, Dan?
	What's happening now. You can title it
	Restoring the Room. Because I like that
	sign on the wall there: Please Restore the Room
	When You Are Finished. It's quantum theory
	really. You know I can't really believe
	in God. I honestly can't imagine
	He'd let all this happen. I have no clue
	if there's an afterlife or what my role
	in this life should be. But there is something
	we don't understand yet. Some things happen
	for a reason. Which is why I wrote you
	back all those years ago when you wrote me
	for no reason. But there was a reason,
	right?
DAN:	Ha ha ha.
JOY:	Okay. Time's up,
DAN:	says Joy.
PAUL:	Are you going to produce Dan's play?
DAN:	asks Paul.
JOY:	It's not really up to me—
DAN:	Ha ha ha!
JOY:	—No no, leave the lights on!
DAN:	says Joy.
PAUL:	—Sorry,
DAN:	says Paul.
PAUL:	Why don't we continue talking
	at the bar next door? Come on, Dan.

DAN: Okay.

Water for me. And then I've got to go
pick up my daughter.   *They exit.*

                                                     The room
has been restored,
lights left on.

                                                     Noise outside
of the next group
arriving.

END OF PLAY